Within your sa....y, ...
and it's now awaiting your beckoning call.

DISCOVER WEALTH
HIDDEN IN YOUR
SALARY

"It is God that giveth thee power to get wealth,
that he may establish his covenant."
Deuteronomy 8:18

Dexter L. Jones
Author of: Hidden Riches of Secret Places

Wasteland Press
Shelbyville, KY USA
www.wastelandpress.net

Discover Wealth Hidden In Your Salary
by Dexter L. Jones

First Printing – June 2006
ISBN13: 978-1-60047-023-3
ISBN10: 1-60047-023-8

Printed in the U.S.A.

Table of Contents

DEDICATION

I dedicate this book to my heavenly Father God, my Lord and Savior Jesus Christ and the Person of the Holy Spirit. I thank God for his continual goodness in allowing me to write books that will bring about a change in the lives of people. Books that are anointed to destroy the yokes and bring about a change in your financial and material life, God wants to prosper you abundantly and this book can show you how to get ahead in the game of finances.

I dedicate this book also to every person that have longed to know what it takes to break the cycle of financial bondage and come into a life of financial increase, prosperity and abundance.

Lastly, I dedicate this book to my darling daughter Jasmine, Daddy loves you and you are my precious one and may all your days be prosperous, successful and full of wealth. 3 John 2

INTRODUCTION

A Sure Word of Prophecy

No one is destined to be poor God has not selected a few to have all the wealth and left the rest to struggle financially for the rest of their lives. He did not choose to bless certain ones without blessing others who will meet the same condition. Acts 10:34

You did not pick up this book by accident, no matter what method it got into your hands you have just encountered destiny, a predetermined event that can change your life if you will listen and obey. In Job 36:11-12 it says, *"If they obey and serve him, they shall spend their days in prosperity, and their years in pleasures. But if they obey not, they shall perish by the sword, and they shall die without knowledge."*

God is for you, he is for you spiritually, physically, financially, materially, mentally, socially, secularly, business, ministry and martially. In every area of your life, God desires that you prosper, excel and succeed in everything that you do. God is magnified in your prosperity and success therefore he wants you to go from glory to glory and advance in everything you pursue. Psalms 35:27 says, *"Let them shout for*

1

joy, and be glad, that favour my righteous cause: yea, let them say continually, Let the LORD be magnified, which hath pleasure in the prosperity of his servant."

If you are a servant of the Lord financial increase and prosperity is your rightful inheritance, you should prosper in life and not to prosper is to live beneath your privilege. This book will show you how to **"Discover Wealth Hidden In Your Salary."**

POTENTIAL

Potential is present but not visible or active power. It's power that lies dormant or inactive, yet within that inactive power lies the ability to make things happen and bring things to pass.

1
THE POTENTIAL WITHIN

*"And God said, Let the earth bring forth grass, the herb yielding seed, and the fruit tree yielding fruit after his kind, **WHOSE SEED IS IN ITSELF**, upon the earth: and it was so." Genesis 1:11*

Within an apple is the potential to make a forest of apple trees the potential is already within the apple to do it. An individual can take the seeds of the apple and cast them aside thereby potentially forfeiting an entire forest of apple trees from coming up, or they can plant the seeds from the apple and start an orchard.

The orchard lies hidden within the apple but the seed is what will bring the orchard forth. The apple is the main object but the seed is the potential, the water and soil helps the seed to come forth and make it capable of producing an apple tree. Yet, God is the one that gives the increase and causes it to flourish.

An apple without seeds cannot produce more apple trees because the potential to do it is gone. Without potential nothing happens yet with potential comes possibilities, potential is latent power or power under the surface that can be manifested to come forth into that which you want to see happen. That which you desire to see happen comes from that which you already have.

- **Potential make things feasible, performable, achievable, accessible and obtainable.**

- **Potential has within it the ability to bring things to pass.**

Miracles vs Prosperity

Throughout the Christian world, many saints are waiting on God to do some miraculous financial miracle on their behalf. God truly is a miracle working God and he performs miraculous miracles both physical and financial but God doesn't want his people to live in a state of waiting on miracles.

God wants you to always have financial increase and prosperity because if he has to continuously perform a miracle in your behalf you're a person that's always in debt and living paycheck to paycheck. You're living in a state of financial chaos and confusion imprisoned by the finances you posses that suppose to be an asset to your life but instead it has become a liability.

Use What You Already Have

God is waiting on the church to allow him to use what they already have. One Sunday while on my way to a teaching engagement the Spirit of the Lord spoke to me and said, **"The blessing of the people, are in the hands of the people."**

For many years, ministers have been trying to get people to give what they don't have. Even to the point of telling individuals to get the finances to give even if they have to borrow it from someone. This isn't the way of God but the way of man God is simply trying to get his people to use what they already have in their possession.

When Jesus performed the miracle of turning the water into wine, he used what the people already had in their possession. At the marriage in Cana of Galilee Jesus mother told him they have no wine, so the story goes, *"And the third day there was a marriage in Cana of Galilee; and the mother of Jesus was there: And both Jesus was called, and his disciples, to the marriage.*

And when they wanted wine, the mother of Jesus

saith unto him, They have no wine. Jesus saith unto her, Woman, what have I to do with thee? Mine hour is not yet come. His mother saith unto the servants, Whatsoever he saith unto you, do it.

And there were set there six waterpots of stone, after the manner of the purifying of the Jews, containing two or three firkins apiece. Jesus saith unto them, Fill the waterpots with water. And they filled them unto the brim. And he saith unto them, Draw out now, and bear unto the governor of the feast. And they bare it.

When the ruler of the feast had tasted the water that was made wine, and knew not whence it was:(but the servant which drew the water knew;) the governor of the feast called the bridegroom, And saith unto him, Every man at the beginning doth set forth good wine; and when men have well drunk, then that which is worse: but thou hast kept the good wine until now.

This beginning of miracles did Jesus in Cana of Galilee, and manifested his glory; and his disciples believed on him. John 2:1-11

Here we see Jesus using what the people already had to perform this miracle he didn't tell the people to borrow any water he used the water that they already had in their possession and performed a miracle.

7

The main object here was the water it was water that was turned into wine, likewise God has placed within your salary all the financial increase you need to lay claim on your wealth.

Discover Wealth Hidden In Your Salary

Another Biblical story that illustrates this truth is Elijah and the widow. Here we have a case of a man of God in need but has a word from the Lord. Also, we have the case of a woman in need that has in her possession everything to sustain her when she puts it in the hand of God.

Famine was in the land the prophet of God was instructed by God to go to the woman to be sustained. The widow woman was gathering sticks and he called her to fetch him some water in a vessel.

As she was going he said, bring me a morsel of bread in thine hand. The woman stated *"I have a handful (**that's more than enough when you trust it to God**) of meal in a barrel and a little oil in a cruse: and me and my son, will eat it and die."*

The prophet of God is now ready to tell her **what you have in your possession is more than enough in the hand of God**. *"For thus saith the*

LORD God of Israel, The barrel of meal shall not waste, neither shall the cruse of oil fail, until the day that the LORD sendeth rain upon the earth. And she, and he and her house, did eat many days." 1 Kings 17:1-16

The widow woman trusted what she already had in the hand of God and it was enough to produce more than she ever imagined.

And what shall I more say? For the time would fail me to tell of the **"fish and loaves Jesus used, the story of Elisha and the woman who oil was multiplied, the drought of fish that was caught by the disciples, the coin in the fishes mouth, the widow that gave two mites etc.** James 6:5-13, 2 Kings 4:1-7, Luke 5:1-9, Matthew 17:24-27, Mark 12:41-44, Luke 2:1-4

God wants to use what you already have in your possession to show you how it can produce financial increase, prosperity and wealth. God's greatest wish for your success is stated in Jeremiah 29:11, *"For I know the thoughts that I think toward you, saith the LORD, thoughts of peace (**safety, wellness, happiness, friendliness, abundance, goodness, health, plenty wholeness and prosperity**), and not of evil (**bad, adversity, affliction, calamity, sorrow and trouble**), to give you and expected end (**a hope, a future and success**)."*

Yet, we see in the life of many Christians more financial calamity and adversity than financial wellness and prosperity. If financial prosperity is God's greatest wish for mankind, then for God to say such a thing without giving man the necessary tools for increase and prosperity is both unsound and unreasonable.

Within this book, you possess the tools necessary to produce the financial increase, prosperity, abundance and wealth that you so deeply long for.

What is it that you financially desire? Is it to have $100's, $1,000's, $10,000's, $100,000's, $1,000,000's or more? The potential to do it is already within your salary. Your salary is the starting point and the main object that can cause it to happen.

Within your salary lies financial increase, prosperity and wealth dormant and inactive, yet within those inactive finances live the ability to make things happen and bring things to pass. Within those inactive finances lives all your financial dreams and financial expectation.

The first step to accomplishing your financial dreams is **realizing** that the financial increase and prosperity you desire you can have it.

It must become a reality to you and a truth conceived in your spirit that your situation shall unquestionably change from what it is to what you desire it to be the realization of this truth has to make such an impression in your spirit and mind that you totally accept it as fact and truth.

Next, you must **believe** that what you set out to achieve financially will certainly come to pass, it shall surely happen. You must then expect this with confidence and become fully persuaded in your mind that nothing and no one can stop it from happening, for "If God be for you, who can be against you." Romans 4:17, Hebrews 11

Last, you must put forth the necessary **effort** or **work** to bring it to pass, to bring it from an idea or thought to a manifested tangible reality before your very eyes. James 2:20-26

Financial increase and prosperity belongs to you dear child of God, it's your inherited right, your family right, your holy right and your born-again right. All that God has belongs to you for you are "heirs of God and joint-heirs with Christ." Romans 8:17

2
DIVINE HELP IN GETTING YOUR WEALTH

"Are they not all ministering spirits, sent forth to minister for them who shall be heirs of salvation."
Hebrews 1:14

In the accumulation of wealth we must realize that God is our source, in 1 Chronicles 29:11-12 David said *"Thine O LORD is the greatness, and the power, and the glory, and the victory, and the majesty: for all that is in the heaven and in the earth is thine; thine is the kingdom, O LORD, and thou art exalted as head above all.*

Both riches and honour come of thee, and thou reignest over all; and in thine hand is power and might; and in thine hand it is to make great, and to give strength unto all."

God in his wisdom has assigned to mankind angels that assist him in his great work. Angels are sent forth to minister on our behalf for we're heirs of salvation and they therefore assist us in our work.

Angels are the divine helpers to assist you in life situations and circumstances.

- **Angels can go before you and prepare your way to make it prosperous. Exodus 23:20-22**
- **Angels can help you prosper in areas of your life. Psalms 91:11-12**
- **Angels can work on your behalf and help bring things to pass. Judges 6:11-22**
- **Angels are sent forth to minister on your behalf. Hebrews 1:14**

The word minister means to serve they will serve you in whatever capacity you need them to help you in, they will not do what you can do but they will help you in what you cannot do.

We have failed to realize the assistance of angels as a result we have omitted the help of God's secret agents.

We do not have the authority or right to charge angels as some teach or tell them what to do this authority and right is assigned to God.

Yet, we see angels in many capacities throughout the scriptures:

- **We see angels as they wait upon Christ. Luke 22:43**
- **We see angels as they help Abraham's servant find a wife for his son Issac. Genesis 24:7, 40**
- **We see an angel speak to Jacob in a dream and give him a business idea of how to prosper. Genesis 31:9-13**
- **We see angels assigned to keep the saints from evil. Psalms 91:10-12**
- **We see how angels are assigned to God's people to bring them into the place God has prepared for them. Exodus 23:20**

Angels are the neglected agents of God that aren't doing a portion of the work they could be doing in the earth because man has failed to realize who they are, what they can do and how they can assist us in life.

You can have divine help in getting your wealth as you ask God to let his angels go forth and minister on your behalf to prosper you in your ways. The angels of God can assist you in many situations and circumstances that may be held back from you by the hand of the enemy.

Angels can help you in finding a job by going before you to prosper your way.

Angels can help you in business by prospering your way and moving upon customers to visit your business or move upon old customers to return.

Angels can speak to man in visions and dreams to direct their steps. Acts 10:3-7, Matthew 2:13

Angels can move upon your boss man to give you that raise that's due you but has been held up by the will of man.

Who knows what has been held up from you that should be yours but satanic forces have blocked your good from coming and you have not asked God to let his angels minister on your behalf to help you.

In the book of Daniel we see how the answer to his prayers were held up by satanic forces that blocked the way from him receiving his answers, but the angels of God assisted Daniel and brought the answer forth.

"Then said he unto me, Fear not, Daniel: for from the first day that thou didst set thine heart to understand, and to chasten thyself before thy God, thy words were heard, and I am come for thy words.

15

But the prince of the kingdom of Persia withstood me one and twenty days: but, lo, Michael, one of the chief princes, came to help me; and I remained there with the kings of Persia.

Now I am come to make thee understand what shall befall thy people in the latter days: for yet the vision is for many days.

Then said he, Knowest thou wherefore I am come unto thee? and now I will return to fight with the prince of Persia: and when I am gone forth, lo, the prince of Grecia shall come." Daniel 10:12-14, 20-21

Angels can give us divine help in many areas of our life where assistance is definitely needed here is a prayer that I like to pray in asking God for divine help in the assistance of angels. You can make it your own.

AFFIRMATION OR PRAYER

"Heavenly Father, I give you praise and thanks for your goodness and mercy. I thank you for being the LORD that exerciseth lovingkindness, judgment and righteousness in the earth. Jeremiah 9:24

I acknowledge you today and I need your help in all things. You said in all our ways to acknowledge you and you will direct our paths. Proverbs 3:6

Father today I ask you to send forth your angels to minister on my behalf for I am an heir of salvation. Father, I am not sufficient of myself as to think anything of myself, but my sufficiency is of thee. 2 Corinthians 3:5

Father, according to your word you have given your angels charge over me to keep me in all my ways, today I need you to let your angels minister on my behalf to _____(here name what you need God to let the angels go forth to do to minister on your behalf) (Example: give me favor in finding a job, help me to sell my product, get new customers, etc.)

Father, I ask you to let your angels go forth now, I desire _____ (Here name what you desire from God) (Example: to find a good paying job, to sell 30 bottles of my product, my business sells to increase, etc.) Mark 11:24

Thank you heavenly father for your blessings now, I believe it and receive it now and I shall have what I desire. Thank you for your faithfulness, for your word will not go out and return void but it shall accomplish that which it was sent to do and it shall prosper therein, in Jesus name Amen. Isaiah 55:11

Now begin to visualize and see yourself receiving that which you have requested of God by faith, see the angels going forth and ministering on your behalf for you're an heir of salvation.

See the angels in your imagination going forth and doing exactly that which you've asked God to send them forth to do. See yourself already in possession of that which you've asked, see yourself doing that which you would do as if your request were answered in reality and you shall have that which you requested.

I make a constant use of this practice in my business and it never fails to bring forth the answer, if I need more customer to call in to make sales I just do as stated above and the calls begin to come in as the angels go forth to minister on my behalf.

If I need more customers to come by to purchase my product, I just go through the affirmation and prayer above and customers begin to come forth and purchase my product.

It's one of the most amazing things as you see it manifested before your eyes and become a reality in your life, many times I have prayed this and within minutes customers have come forth to buy the product.

It's time to get divine help in getting your wealth as you ask God to let his angels minister in your behalf for you're an heir of salvation.

3
THE POWER TO THINK

"Finally, brethren, whatsoever things are true, whatsoever things are honest, whatsoever things are just, whatsoever things are pure, whatsoever things are lovely, whatsoever things are of good report; if there be any virtue; if there be any praise, think on these things." Philippians 4:8

The one idea I want to convey to you in this chapter relates to the thoughts in your mind on a daily basis. As a society we have failed to realize the power of our thoughts we've failed to realize that the thoughts which dominate our thinking has a direct correlation and connection with the things that we experience in our life.

Here are six of the most powerful words that I can relate to you that can change your life and cause a complete metamorphosis in every area.

WE BECOME WHAT WE THINK ABOUT

Where you are right now in your life is a result of the thoughts that have continually dominated your thinking. Here, I want to reemphasize various points that I accentuated in the book **"Hidden Riches of Secret Places"** because these points are too vital to go unnoticed.

- You cannot wish, hope and desire financial increase and then have thoughts of poverty, lack, barely making ends meet and living paycheck to paycheck dominating your thought life.

- Either one thought pattern or the other will dominate your mind and produce results in accordance with the dominating thoughts you're thinking.

- *"For as he (man) thinketh in his heart, so is he." Proverbs 23:7* You can't think one way and then expect another way to come forth the thoughts you're sowing in your mind you will reap in your life and there's no way around it. You will become what you think.

- You need to get this scripture in your spirit so it can become a revelation in your heart.

You must come into the knowledge that your thoughts are what you, your finances and your life will become. There is no exception to this rule you will become the dominating thoughts that you're thinking.

There is a universal law in the realm of the mind that works the same for all mankind, that law is **"like attract like," "cause and effect," "what you sow, you will reap,"** and **"everything produces after its kind."** Genesis 1:11-12 An apple tree cannot produce oranges nor can a pecan tree produce plums every tree only produces after its kind. Luke 6:43-44

What you must do is begin to renew your mind, as a Christian you have been given a new spirit the Spirit of God dwells in your spirit causing your spirit to be alive towards God. Ezekiel 36:26

However, the majority of Christians have failed to renew their minds, God will not renew your mind he has left this task in the hands of each believer and many have done nothing to renew their minds.

The scriptures plainly tells us to *"Be not*

conformed to this world (this worlds way of negative thinking) but be ye transformed (changed, transfigured, a complete meta-morphosis) by the renewing (the renovating, the tearing down and away) of your mind, that ye may prove what is that good, and acceptable and perfect will of God." Romans 12:2-3

Many time people go into prayer lines to get ministers to pray for their situation to change, what needs to change is your thinking, ministers need to pray that your thinking change from what it is to what it needs to be.

- Your thinking needs to change from failure consciousness to success consciousness. Joshua 1:8

- Your thinking needs to change from poverty consciousness to wealth consciousness. Deuteronomy 8:18

- Your thinking needs to change from sickness to health. 3 John 2

- Your thinking needs to change from lack and barely making ends meet to abundance and opulence. Deuteronomy 28:1-14

- Your thinking needs to change from I can't to *"I can do all things through Christ which strengthens me." Philippians 4:13*

There is nothing true, honest, just, pure, lovely, of good report, of virtue or of praise about or in reference to:

*poverty * lack * sin * barely making ends meet * sickness * confusion * unforgiveness * paycheck to paycheck living * evil works

From this day forward change your way of thinking and begin to think relevant to the word of God for what you think soon affects your spirit and anything that gets in your spirit whether negative or positive, good or bad is a thousand times stronger than any thing in your mind.

When something good gets into your spirit then you're able to see the impossible take place and miraculous things begins to happen in your life right before your eyes.

1 You will be able to say to the mountains in your life *"Be thou removed, and be thou cast into the sea; and it shall be done. And all things, whatsoever ye shall ask in prayer, believing shall be done." Matthew 21:21-22*

2 You will be able to tell the fig tree (your life situations) *"No man eat of thee*

hereafter for ever. And presently the fig tree will whither away." Matthew 21:19-20, Mark 11:12-14

3   You will be able to *"Launch out into the deep, and let down your nets (businesses, plans) for a draught. And enclose a great multitude of fishes (customers for your businesses)." Luke 5:4-9*

4   You will be able to *"turn water into wine (turn something natural into something of great value)." St. John 2:1-11*

It all begins with the power to think, most individuals only have mental assent or mental agreement with the word of God, there is no power in this the power is when that word becomes alive in your spirit and from there it affects your entire life.

Your thoughts create your circumstances and lifestyle. Your thoughts create images and the image which you consistently hold in your mind will produce for you according to the image held.

Man is not a creature of conditions but instead creates his conditions by his dominating thoughts.

In essence, what you think you will soon become

"For as he (man) thinketh in his heart so is he."
Proverbs 23:7 As he continues to think so he continues to be.

The dominating thoughts of your mind that's hidden from others will attract to you the environment and circumstance which your thoughts secretly longs for whether good or bad.

We know what you're thinking by the circumstance and situations that surrounds your life if you're dissatisfied with the picture your life is portraying to others and the witness you're being for God then change it by simply changing your thinking.

Begin to see yourself not as you are but visualize yourself as if you were what you want to be, you can do this by meditation.

Here are two scriptures and a method of meditation that can bring increase, prosperity and wealth into your life.

*"But thou shalt remember the LORD thy God: for it is he that giveth thee power to get **wealth,** that he may establish his covenant which he sware unto the fathers, as it is this day."*
Deuteronomy 8:18

"This book of the law shall not depart out of thy

*mouth; but thou shalt meditate therein day and night, that thou mayest observe to do according to all that is written therein: for then thou shalt make thy way **prosperous**, and then thou shalt have good **success**." Joshua 1:8*

Here is what to do to get increase, prosperity and wealth coming into your life: Go into a quite place and begin to meditate on these scriptures start with the first one in Deuteronomy 8:18, repeat this scripture aloud two or three times, then take out the word **wealth** and begin to affirm this word over and over again many times.

Afterward imagine yourself in wealthy situations such as a large check amount made out to you, large deposits being made in your checking account, unexpected money coming to you in large amounts. This will have a powerful effect on your mind and your spirit.

Next, do the same with the second scripture in Joshua 1:8, repeat this scripture aloud two or three times, then take out the word **prosperous** or **success** which ever you prefer and begin to affirm this word over and over again.

Likewise, see yourself in your imagination in successful and prosperous situations where you're accomplishing a task that you desire to achieve, or see yourself reaching a goal that you've set for yourself. Imagine it in detail see the surroundings, feel it, smell it, touch it, hear it, let it be so real that you can taste it's outcome.

Do each of these exercise for about five to ten minutes a day two to three times a day and watch the effects of what will begin to happen in your life, you will notice increase, prosperity and wealth becoming a reality before your eyes.

"Meditate upon these things; give thyself wholly to them; that thy profiting may appear to all." 1 Timothy 4:15

4
THE SALARY

"In all labour there is profit." Proverbs 14:23

"Love not sleep, lest thy come to poverty; open thine eyes, and thou shalt be satisfied with bread. Yet a little sleep, a little slumber, a little folding of the hands to sleep: So shall thy poverty come as one that travelleth; and thy want as an armed man. How long wilt thy sleep, O sluggard? When wilt thou arise out of thy sleep: For the desire of the slothful killeth him; for his hands refuse to labour. But he that gathereth by labour shall increase. For the soul of the diligent shall be made fat." Proverbs 24:33-34, 20:13, 21:25, 13:4, 11

A man's salary is the wages that he receives for his services it is payment for work rendered. In olden times, men worked and received other things for wages instead of money.

- Some received animals, food, clothing etc. but today the general wages for work rendered is money.

- Money is also the number one medium of exchange used today in relations to purchasing goods.

- Without available money, mankind is limited in what he can do and what he can purchase, with a full supply of money he is unlimited in his purchasing power and his ability to do.

- If you want to have money the only right and legal method of getting it is by work.

- Work will cause you to have money and money will give you a salary or a wage for work done. No work, no salary, no salary no money no money no ability to do things and no purchasing power.

If you want to discover wealth you must first have a salary in order for it to be revealed with the method and truth we're referring to here. For wealth lies hidden in your salary, in the beginning of acquiring increase, prosperity and wealth it has no bearing on the size of your salary.

Wealth is not accumulated over night and there's no such thing as overnight riches, no such thing as get rich quick. All things requires work and time, if you will put forth the necessary effort (work) with the proper knowledge and give it enough time with God's help you can bring any kind of venture to pass.

Our Main Focus

Our main focus in this book is your salary, it's the salary that gives God and you something to work with and work through. I'll define salary as any kind of income that you have coming to you on a weekly, bi-weekly or monthly basis.

1 Whether it's a government check, regular job, social security, child support, income from your son, daughter, husband, or business, if you have access to a steady stream of income we will define this as your salary.

2 Salaries differ from one another but the fact that you have a salary puts everyone on equal ground. Whether the salary is $1000 a week, or $100 a week both individuals will be able to discover wealth that's hidden there.

Without A Salary

A question may be asked in reference to salary stating what shall I do if I have no salary but desire to discover wealth that God has for me.

The first thing you must realize is that in this day and time God always has something that he works with and work through.

When Jesus performed the prosperity miracle of turning water into wine he used what they already had to perform the miracle, he didn't make wine out of thin air (*even though he could have*) he used the water that was available to make the wine.

When he fed the multitude with two fishes and five loaves he used those available sources to feed the multitude, once again he didn't produce fish and loaves out of thin air.

This is God's normal method of operation that he uses to perform his acts. Therefore having no salary gives God nothing to work with unless he chooses to supersede his normal plan of action and perform a miracle in your behalf out of his goodness and mercy.

If God refuse to break his pattern or method then you will have to reap the consequences of lack, poverty and barely making ends meet because you have not wisely positioned yourself to lay claim on wealth.

Nevertheless, you can position yourself and refuse to live in the above manner regardless of where you are at the moment so that you can get where you need to be to fulfill the financial destiny that God has ordained for your life as a child of God.

If you're presently without a salary of any kind, what you need to do is pray and ask the Lord to open a door for you to get a job, start a business or to receive some type of public assistance if you're unable to work. This is also an opportunity to use divine help (angels) to get your wealth.

God wants you to work don't fool yourself into believing that God will supply your needs and you will not have to work in order to have money, this is a lie from Satan to keep you in poverty and lack disabling you from acquiring the abundant life God has for you.

- You must have some type of income coming in to live, in 2 Thessalonians 3:10 it says, *"If any would not work, neither should he eat."* Simply put God is saying if you refuse to work and you can work you should starve, you don't deserve any of life's pleasures or financial and material blessing because you refuse to work in order to get them.

- In 1 Thessalonians 4:11 it says, *"And that ye study to be quiet, and to do your own business, and to **work with your own hands,** as we commanded you."*

Yet, if you really want a salary to lay claim on your increase, prosperity and wealth, go to God in sincerity and humility and ask him to open a door of opportunity for you to get income coming in so you can work and make money. God knows where the jobs are and the public assistance that you need to help you get ahead in the game of life.

Stating to God it's your desire to have a salary so that you can bring your tithes and offerings in the house of God, make money for you and your family, be a blessing to others and enjoy life. God wants you to have increase and prosperity more than you can ever imagine and even more than you desire to have increase and prosperity.

The scriptures states, *"Therefore I say unto you, What things soever ye desire, when ye pray, believe that ye receive them, and ye shall have them. Ask, and it shall be given you; seek, and ye shall find; knock, and it shall be opened. Or what man is there of you, whom if his son ask bread, will he give him a stone?*

Or if he ask a fish, will he give him a serpent? If ye then, being evil, know how to give good gifts unto your children, how much more shall your Father which is in heaven give good things to them that ask him? Mark 11:24-26, Matthew 7:7-11

You must have a salary of some sort in order to discover the wealth that's there and put these principles that you will learn in this book into action. Begin today to seek the Lord and watch God work on your behalf.

When God open for you that door of opportunity don't forget God and begin to enjoy the blessings more than the blesser.

If you already have a salary of any kind you're in good shape financially, you already have what you need to change your situation and circumstances and begin a new financial future.

For within your salary God has placed your increase, prosperity and wealth and it's now awaiting your beckoning call as the following chapters show you how to make it work for you instead of against you.

5
YOU MUST DO SOMETHING DIFFERENT

"Prepare thy work without, and make it fit for thyself
in the field: and afterwards build thine house."
Proverbs 24:27

If you want something that you've never had, then you must do something that you've never done. If you keep repeating the same process, you're going to keep getting the same results you can't expect different results following the same pattern.

If you want different results than what you've had in the past, then you must choose a different course of action for the future. It's all in the power of your choice.

You're where you are today as a result of the choices that you've made yesterday(s). Some of your choices were bad some were good, whether bad or good you're where you are as a result of them.

The clothes you wear, the car you drive, the church you attend, the job you work, the salary you have, your wife or husband, all are the result of your choices.

THE DIFFERENCE THAT MAKES THE DIFFERENCE

At any time, you can change any of the choices you've made and the change will produce for you a different set of results that you will have to deal with.

- You are not bound to the life you're currently experiencing if you're unhappy in any area, you can change it by simply choosing a different course of action.

- If you're not happy with your current financial status, you can change it if you're willing to make both mental and natural changes.

- If the course of action you're currently following isn't bringing you closer to your fortune and financial goal then you need to do something different than what you're doing.

- You can't keep doing business the same old way and expect different results.

- Taking a different course of action doesn't have to be anything drastic but it must be something different than what you're doing now.

As an example let us observe one idea that we'll elaborate on more in the other chapters, If you having been trying to save up $1000 but have not been successful you must begin to take a different course of action to save that $1000.

One course of action may be to begin taking out 10% of your income and put it into a savings account and refuse to touch it for any reason, if you can't put aside 10% then begin with 5%.

The idea is to begin taking a different course of action and begin it now. I remember once when I was on a mission to save up one thousand dollars in a savings it seemed that I could not save up a thousand dollars for nothing.

I was trying to save it up by doing the same old things that I had been doing in the past yet expecting a different result, however there was no different result that came forth for me simply because I wasn't taking a different course of action.

One day I decided to do something different to help me reach my goal of saving a thousand dollars, this different course of action was by no means easy but thank God, I realized that if I wanted something different then I must do something different.

So I begin to sacrificially take out fifty dollars a week or 10% of my income, fifty dollars that I did not have but if I wanted to reach my goal I had to do this in spite of my situation and circumstances.

- As a result of my different course of action, I was able to save the one thousand dollars and this was the beginning of my financial increase.

- As you will learn in this book, money of itself is neither good nor bad, it's the thoughts that follow the money that makes it either good or bad.

- Also, with money it's not how much you have that's important but how you manage what you have that's the key to financial increase and prosperity.

Nothing happened for me until I begin to take a different course of action only then did I begin to get the results that I had been seeking for quite some time.

- If you want more than you've had in the past then you must go further than where you've been.

- If you want to reap a different financial harvest then you must begin to plant different financial seeds.

Your financial future is wrapped up in the choices that you will make from this day forward.

Refuse to allow your next three years to be like your past three years, however good or bad they were it can be better.

You are the one that can make it better God gave you the power of choice and you have the authority to change it and make it better, your future is in your hands.

6
THE TITHES

"Bring ye all the tithes into the storehouse, that there may be meat in mine house, and prove me now herewith, saith the LORD of hosts, if I will not open you the windows of heaven, and pour you out a blessing, that there shall not be room enough to receive it." Malachi 3:10

God has made great and precious promises to his people the tithes are God's way that he has given for his people to get in on his blessings. To get the prosperity of God working in your life you must be obedient to the word of God. The scripture states, *"If ye be willing and obedient, ye shall eat the good of the land: But if ye refuse and rebel, ye shall be devoured with the sword: for the mouth of the LORD hath spoken it." Isaiah 1:19-20*

- The one obedient call that God is making to his people is a return to him in bringing their tithes and offering to the house of God.

41

- God's plan of tithing is the best method given to get man on the road to financial increase, prosperity and wealth.

However, when God's plan of tithing is neglected it causes mankind to be devoured in his situation and circumstances by the very word of God that promises his blessings.

If you will receive God's plan of tithing, you will wisely position yourself to be able to eat the good of the land and experience financial increase, prosperity and wealth.

If you refuse to obey God's plan of tithing, you will not prosper and you will experience financial lack, bondage and poverty, not only will your financial life decline but also many other areas of your life will begin to suffer.

God is able and willing to allow you and I to have as much wealth as we will determine to use to glorify his name, extend his kingdom and be a blessing. In the process of building up God's kingdom the word of God states that, *"God has given us richly all things to enjoy." 1 Timothy 6:17*

THE SERIOUSNESS OF THE TITHES

In Malachi, we find God speaking to the children of Israel concerning the tithes and offering, they had gotten away from bringing the tithes and offering to the house of God.

As a result, they were being devoured in many areas of their life, so God spoke to them through the prophet Malachi saying, *"Return unto me, and I will return unto you, saith the LORD of hosts."* Malachi 3:7

1 The reason why God is so adamant about bringing the tithes is because the tithes, is a basic admission that **"God is man's source"** and not man's money or resources.

2 The tithes was to be consistently brought as an indication that it all belonged to God and as a recognition of the place of priority that God holds in the life of man.

In the mind of God, as long as this one area is neglected there could be no true relationship between God and man, because how can you truly worship and obey God while you're robbing him at the same time. Malachi 3:8

God is very adamant about this because nothing that we do makes up for our disobedience in this area.

1   If we put away the sin and wrongdoing and begin to live a life of holiness and righteousness.

2   If we become more faithful in our church services.

3   If we spend more time in prayer and in the word.

None of these things make up for not bringing the tithes. Such thing we ought to do they are our reasonable service and what Christian people are supposed to do, **yet that one neglected command still makes us robbers in the eyes of God.**

Until the body of Christ gets it right in this area no other areas of obedience can compensate for our departure from the tithes and offering.

However, if we will obey in this area, God will bless us and enable us to eat the good of the land, and God has promised to open the windows of heaven and pour us out a blessing that we shall not have room enough to receive it.

We should make it priority number 1 to get the windows of heaven open over our life, this allows God to release to us what we need most in order to have financial increase, prosperity and wealth.

In the time of the Israelites God gave to them what they needed most in order to increase and prosper, the Israelites were agricultural people who lived off the land.

What they needed most was rain, when God promised to open the windows of heaven for them he promised to give them the rain that was needed for their crops to grow so that they could experience a harvest of increase. Leviticus 26:4, Deuteronomy 11:13-17, 28:12

The tithes rightly belong to God and he has entrusted you and I to faithfully bring it to his house. When we obey God, this allows him to release the vast treasures in the storehouse of heaven and get heaven's resources into our life.

A RETURN TO TITHING

God is calling his people to return to him in bringing the tithes and offerings the people of God in Malachi's day had departed from God's ordinances, doubted the value of serving God and distrusted his ability to care for them. As a result, they ceased bringing the tithes and offering.

Yet, God in his grace and mercy takes the initiative to call them back to him saying, *"Return unto me."* Malachi 3:7 God delights in giving man the opportunity to experience the blessing of walking under an open heaven.

As saints of God we don't need the blessing of receiving natural rain for crops because we're not agricultural people, today the blessing of walking under an open heaven gives us the opportunity to receive what we need most to prosper, wisdom and understanding. Proverbs 4:5-9

Walking under an open heaven gives God the opportunity to allow us to look into those windows that he promised to open up and also give us the opportunity to see in the realm of the spirit and receive revelations.

God will impart to us spiritual truths and nuggets of revelation knowledge, "that the spirit of wisdom and revelation in the knowledge of Christ may rest upon us. The eyes of your understanding being enlightened; that ye may know what is the hope of his calling, and what the riches of the glory of his inheritance in the saints, And what is the exceeding greatness of his power to us-ward who believe, according to the working of his mighty power. Ephesians 1:17-19

The tithes is our starting point it shows God that we recognize his ownership and possession of all things for the tithes belongs to him and it's our reasonable service to obey.

- Bringing the tithes lets God know that he can trust us with financial substance.

- This is an important step toward discovering wealth hidden in your salary if you can get it correct here God will empower you financially.

If you miss it here you miss it everywhere, you cannot sensibly expect God to bless you financially while you rob him financially.

Tithing is a biblical principal that's based on the word of God stating, *"If you will honor God with a tenth of your income God will in return honor you with increase, prosperity and abundance."*

The tenth that you bring to God's storehouse shows gratitude to God the creator for allowing you to possess a portion of the creator's resources that rightfully belongs to the creator.

God only ask for a tenth of your income so that their will be resources in his house to get his work done. When you honor God by first giving him a tenth it shows him that you honor him above the things of life.

As a result, God will give you the things of life in abundance. When you follow the principal of tithing God gives the increase and causes the ninety percent left over to increase and flourish.

As a result, of your obedience God will give you that which you need most to use the ninety percent left over with keenness and intelligence, he gives you wisdom and understanding. Proverbs 8:11-21

When you follow the principal of tithing faithfully God looks down upon you with special favor and honors you financially for honoring him financially.

Tithing puts God on your side and allows him to work in your behalf in a marvelous way. Proverbs 3:9-10 says, *"Honour the LORD with thy substance, and with the **firstfruits of all thine increase**: So shall thy barns be filled with plenty, and thy presses shall burst out with new wine."*

As you consistently follow the principal of tithing, you will begin to see the marvelous works of God in your financial life and other areas of your life as well.

You will begin to notice that you're able to do more with the remaining ninety percent than you were with the hundred percent that you kept all for yourself.

Let's observe an example of how to take out the tithes from your income so that no one will be confused about the amount. If your income is $200 you will take out a tenth of that which totals $20, you will bring this to the house of God as your tithes.

In doing this, you're honoring God first with your finances and allowing God to get involved in your situations and circumstance and to bless the work of your hand.

Honoring God first with the tithes show faith and trust in God.

- It proclaims that you're looking to God as your source in life.

- It proclaims him as the God of your faith.

- It proclaims him as the one who is the possessor of heaven and earth and able to do exceedingly above all you can ask or think.

- It proclaims him as the God of miracles,

abundance, possibilities and the Almighty God.

- The one who gives Divine provision, Divine supply, and increase to those that put their trust in him.

- It proclaims tithing as God's way for his children and his means of opening the windows of heaven in their behalf.

If you would trust God by bringing the tithes into his house, you will begin to experience a closeness, which the disobedient will never have. Tithing is God's way!

7
TRUSTING GOD

"But my God shall supply all your need according to his riches in glory by Christ Jesus." Philippians 4:19

In order to operate in God's plan of economy we must come to the conclusion that **God is our source**. The word economy is defined as a system of producing and dividing wealth. It deals with our natural economy. The sad reality is that we focus more upon the natural system of wealth than the spiritual system of wealth.

God indeed has a plan of economy and his plan is miraculous in nature. It's spiritual and has a spiritual basis. As children of God, we must understand that our main focus should be God's plan of economy and not mainly the economy of the world.

In the regular or natural operation of things 2 fishes and 5 loaves feeds maybe 1 or 2 people, in

51

God's miraculous plan of operation 2 fishes and 5 loaves fed 5000 men besides women and children with 12 baskets left over. *Matthew 14:14-21*

1   God has a 3-fold purpose to fulfill in the earth first he has to get meat in his house so that his work will be taken care of.

2   Second, he has to make sure that his Apostles, Prophets, Evangelists, Pastors and Teachers are taken care of, *"Even so hath the Lord ordained that they which preach the gospel should live of the gospel." 1 Corinthians 9:7-13, 14*

3   Third, he has to make sure that his people that serve him have what they need to take care of their families and also to enjoy life. *Malachi 3:10, Ephesians 4:7-14, 1 Timothy 5:17-18, Nehemiah 2, Exodus 25-28, Ecclesiastes 2:24, 3:13, 5:18*

The reason we don't see miraculous manifestations in the financial realm more is because we're focusing more upon what we can do than what God can do with what we have.

We're living more according to our own riches and resources than God's riches and resources as a result we're only able to do what we can do instead of what God can do.

God is ready and willing to do more financially in the lives of his people in the way of financial increase, prosperity and wealth. In order for God to get money into the hands of his people, he must first get money out of the hands of his people.

There is plenty of money in this world and God knows where it is and how to get it. In Job 22:23-25 it says, *"If thou return to the Almighty, thou shalt be built up, thou shalt put away iniquity far from thy tabernacles. Then shalt **thou lay up gold as dust**, and the gold of Ophir as the stones of the brooks. Yea, the Almighty shall be thy defence, and thou shalt **have plenty of silver.**"*

God needs wealth in circulation and he wants you to circulate it for him. God will allow you to have as much wealth as you'll use for his glory and the good of mankind.

- Can God trust you with wealth? Are you using the money that you currently have in your possession for him by bringing the tithes and offerings into his storehouse? If you will not trust him now with what you have, neither will you trust him with wealth if he gives it to you.

For *"He that is faithful in that which is least is faithful also in much: and he that is unjust in the*

53

least is unjust also in much." Luke 16:10

God wants you to be free from the love of money so that he can bless you with more money. The individual that loves money is operating by a spirit of greed and has made money their god. For *"He that loveth silver shall not be satisfied with silver; nor he that loveth abundance with increase. For the love of money is the root of all evil: which while some coveted after, they have erred from the faith, and pierced themselves through with many sorrows." Ecclesiastes 5:10, 1 Timothy 6:10*

The three things that can keep you from enjoying God's riches are greed, doubt and fear. Greed is defined as the desire to acquire and keep more than one needs. Greed is equated with idolatry and covetousness. Greed defines one character and a person motivated by greed will be motivated by love for one's self and will sacrifice God and others to possess thing.

An example of this is the rich young ruler in *Luke 18:18-30*, this young man refused to let go of his money and in the end lost his money and missed out on the call of Jesus.

Holding money from God can keep you from the best that God has for you and cause you to miss out on the true riches of life. *Matthew 6:24, Luke 12:15, 16:11-13, 1 Corinthians 5:11*

- Our motivation must be a love for God and the love of God. A person motivated by love for God will sacrifice money and things in order to see God's work done and others blessed.

- When a person is motivated by greed and selfishness doubt and unbelief puts up a constant battle to get them to disbelieve the word of God and distrust the way of God.

When Jesus came to his own country with his disciples he wanted to do some mighty works there but the scriptures says, *"Jesus said unto them, A prophet is without honor, but in his own country, and among his own kin, and in his own house. **And he could there do no mighty work, save that he laid his hands upon a few sick folk, and healed them. And he marveled because of their unbelief.** And he went about the villages teaching." Mark 6:4-6*

If you want to get in on God's plan of economy and begin to live according to his riches and resources then you must get rid of doubt and unbelief. Hearing the word of God and speaking the word of God will get rid of doubt and unbelief in your life.

Since Jesus couldn't do many mighty works in his own country, he went about teaching the word to get the people to hear so that faith could come. *"So then faith cometh by hearing, and hearing by the word of God." Romans 10:17*

Until you learn to trust God with what you have you'll never see the mighty works of God in your behalf, begin to throw yourself wholehearted on God trusting him every step of the way and watch him move on your behalf.

Trusting God with what you have in your possession is the stepping-stone to get God to trust you with more. In Proverbs 3:5-6 it says, *"Trust in the LORD with all thine heart; and lean not unto thine own understanding. In all thy ways acknowledge him, and he shall direct your paths."*

In the beginning you may not even remotely understand this thing about trusting God, your bills may be insurmountable, your money at a minimum, but if you will lean not to your own understanding and put what you have in God's hand he shall direct your paths.

"Honour the LORD with thy substance, and with the firstfruits of all thine increase: So shall thy barns be filled with plenty, and thy presses shall burst out with new wine." Proverbs 3:9-10

God wants to deliver you out of the hands of all your enemies an enemy of both God and mankind is poverty. You're not destined to live in lack and barely making ends meet but if you refuse to trust God you're setting yourself up to be overtaken by your enemies.

David was a man that understood what it meant to trust God and he realized that trusting God was the key to deliverance from his enemies. In 2 Samuel 22:1-7, 20, 29-31 it says, *"David spake unto the LORD the words of this song, in the day that the LORD had delivered him out of the hand of all his enemies, and out of the hand of Saul:*

And he said, The LORD is my rock, and my fortress, and my deliverer; The God of my rock, in him will I trust: he is my shield, and the horn of my salvation, my high tower, and my refuge, my saviour; thou savest me from violence.

I will call on the LORD, who is worthy to be praised: so shall I be saved from mine enemies. When the waves of death compassed me, the flood of ungodly men made me afraid; The sorrows of hell compassed me about; the snares of death prevented me;

In my distress I called upon the LORD, and cried to my God: and he did hear my voice out of his temple, and my cry did enter into his ears. He

*brought me forth also into a large place: he
delivered me, because he delighted in me.*

*For thou art my lamp, O LORD: and the LORD
will lighten my darkness. For by thee I have run
through a troop: by my God have I leaped over a
wall. As for God, his way is perfect; the word of
the LORD is tried: he is a buckler to all them
that trust in him."*

Somewhere along the way David learned to trust
in God he realized that his battles in life could be
won much easier by submitting to God and his
ways.

Likewise your financial battle and all your life
battles is not yours but the Lord's, you have
already been given the victory in every situation
but you must trust God to work in you and
through you.

When David fought Goliath, he realized that he
could not beat this giant with sword and spear but
he must put his trust in the LORD and go forth
into battle.

*"Then said David to the Philistine, Thou comest
to me with a sword, and with a spear, and with a
shield: but I come to thee in the name of the
LORD of hosts, the God of the armies of Israel,
whom thou hast defied.*

*This day will the LORD deliver thee into mine hand **(look at his trust in God)**; and I will smite thee, and take thine head from thee; and I will give the carcasses of the host of the Philistines this day unto the fowls of the air, and to the wild beasts of the earth; that all the earth may know that there is a God in Israel.*

*And all this assembly shall know that the LORD saveth not with sword and spear: **for the battle is the LORD's, he will give you into our hands.**" 1 Samuel 17:45-47*

This day set your mind and heart in position to trust in the living God when you do this you show forth your trust in God by obeying his word and doing that which he has asked of you with the right motive.

"Be not afraid nor dismayed by reason of this great multitude (your financial crisis, financial dilemma or the financial opposition that you may be experiencing at the moment); for the battle is not yours, but God's.

Ye shall not need to fight in this battle: set yourselves, stand ye still, and see the salvation of the LORD with you, O Judah and Jerusalem (O Saints of God): fear not, nor be dismayed; to morrow go out against them (your financial situations): for the LORD will be with you." 2 Chronicles 20:15-17 **See our books "Hidden Riches of Secret Places" and "Money Answers All Things"**

"For we walk by faith, not by sight."
2 Corinthians 5:7

8
THE POWER OF GIVING

"Give and it shall be given unto you; good measure, pressed down, and shaken together, and running over, shall men give into your bosom. For with the same measure that ye mete withal it shall be measured to you again." Luke 6:38

Many times in life, we greatly desire to receive but the key to receiving is understanding that, *"it is more blessed to give than to receive." Acts 20:35*

God does not have a problem with us desiring to receive for he admonishes us to have an attitude of expectation according to the gospel of Mark 11:24 saying, *"Therefore I say unto you, What things soever ye desire, when ye pray, believe that **ye receive them**, and ye shall have them."*

According to our beginning verse Luke 6:38 our receiving is based upon the measure of our giving. For you cannot give without receiving but the measure you receive will be in accordance with the measure of your giving.

Notice that the verse does not begin with **"receive and it shall be given"** but **give and it shall be given**, denoting that you start the receiving in motion by your giving not your receiving.

Throughout the Bible we see the power of giving in action, and every place where giving has been done the receiving from that which was given has come forth in a greater measure than the amount that was given.

The greatest measure of giving we see exemplified was when God gave his son, in St. John 3:16 it says, *"For God so loved the world, that **he gave** his only begotten Son, that whosoever believeth in him should not perish, but have everlasting life."*

• When God gave his son he was in **expectation of receiving** many sons back from the one and only begotten son that he gave. God did not give his son without expecting to receive any sons back.

• When you give, you must not only give from the heart but you must give with an expectation to receive from the giving that you gave. If you give expecting nothing then you will receive nothing, God never told man to give without an expectation of return.

As a result, of God giving his only begotten son the scriptures says that, *"For it became him, for whom are all things, and by whom are all things, in bringing many sons unto glory." Hebrews 2:10a*

God's one son has produced for him many sons, *"Behold, what manner of love the Father hath bestowed upon us, that we should be called the* **sons** *of God, therefore the world knoweth us not, because it knew him not. Beloved, now are we the* **sons** *of God." 1 John 3:1-2a*

God did not keep back his only begotten son he gave his only son and today you and I are sons, Hallelujah, Praise the Lord!

Until you learn the power of giving, what could have been yours you will never receive because you refuse to let go of what you had that you might receive what was yours.

When you learn to give of your finances you open the gates for more finances to come forth, when you refuse to give of your finances the very finances that you have will imprison you financially and lock the gate so that more finances cannot come in.

You can give in many ways, financially, you can give offering along with your tithes you can give towards causes that help others by supporting charities and other organizations. When you give, God will bless you because you are operating by the very heart of God.

HOW TO LEND MONEY TO GOD

If you want to let your money work for you instead of against you the best way to do it is put it in the hand of God. When you give of your finances to help the poor you are lending money to God according to the scriptures.

"He that hath pity upon the poor lendeth unto the LORD; and that which he hath given will he pay him again." Proverbs 19:17

One of the best ways to give money is to give to help the poor, there are many scriptures that emphasize what happens when you give of your substance to help the poor.

"He that hath a bountiful eye shall be blessed; for he giveth of his bread to the poor." Proverbs 22:9

"He that giveth unto the poor shall not lack; but he that hideth his eyes shall have many a curse." Proverbs 28:27

"The King that faithfully judgeth the poor, his throne shall be established for ever." Proverbs 29:14

"If there be among you a poor man of one of thy brethern within thy gates in thy land which the LORD giveth thee, thou shalt not harden thine heart, nor shut thine hand from thy poor brother: But thou shalt open thine hand wide unto him, and shalt surely lend him sufficient for his need, in that which he wanteth. Thou shalt surely give him, and thine heart shalt not be grieved when thou givest unto him: because that for this thing the LORD thy God shall bless thee in all thy works, and in all that thou puttest thine hand unto." Deuteronomy 15:7-8, 10

"He that by usury and unjust gain increaseth his substance, he shall gather it for him that will pity the poor." Proverbs 28:8

When you give money to the poor you are putting God in debt to you and God pays all his bills. The problem today is that not many people are lending to God by helping the poor.

The poor is not the lazy, slothful, sluggard etc.,

65

the poor are those that are unable to help themselves or those that have truly fallen on hard times and need some financial assistance for the moment. There are many worthy causes that you can support that needs financial assistance.

Seek the Lord about the right causes to support that helps the poor or find individuals that you know that aren't slothful but have just fallen on hard times.

Within your salary is money that should be used to help the poor, this money can come from using just 2% of your salary to help those in need. Example: if your salary is 300 a week, 2% of that is $6 a week or just $24 a month to give to the poor.

What I want you to understand here is that the sum of money that you will be using from your salary to create financial increase, prosperity and wealth can be simply one quarter out of every dollar in this manner:

1. 10% is given for tithes, one dime.

2. 10% is used to pay yourself, one dime.

3. A percentage should be used for an offering, let's say you choose to give 3% for an offering, three cents.

4. A percentage should be used to help the poor, let's say you choose to give 2%, two cents.

You have given a total of twenty five cents out of your salary to create your increase, prosperity and wealth. Take the initiative to lend to God and get him in debt to you and you will experience the financial success that you desire.

"Give, and it shall be given unto you; good measured, pressed down, and shaken together, and running over, shall men give unto your bosom. For with the same measure ye mete withal it shall be measured to you again." Luke 6:38

"There is that scattereth, and yet increaseth; and there is that withholdeth more than is meet, but it tendeth to poverty. The liberal soul shall be made fat: and he that watereth shall be watereth also himself." Proverbs 11:24-25

9
TITHE TO YOURSELF

"Go to the ant, thou sluggard; consider her ways, and be wise: Which having no guide, overseer, or ruler, Provideth her meat in the summer, and gathereth her food in the harvest." Proverbs 6:6-8

Tithing to yourself is an idea that's rarely heard of in the church it's a principle that will bring about financial increase when it's performed with wisdom and continuity.

The word tithe or tithing is only heard of in reference to bringing the tithes off of your income so that there will be meat in God's house. Malachi 3:10

However in the same manner that you give to God so that there will be substance in his house you can likewise give to yourself so that you can have substance in your house.

Individuals rarely think of taking a portion of their money and paying themselves just as faithful as they would pay their bills or bring their tithes.

Tithing to yourself is based on the principle of taking a tenth of your salary and putting it aside for you. This is money that you will use to build your fortune and bring about financial increase, prosperity and abundance in your life.

- Most individuals take their salary and pay everyone but themselves but when you learn the value of tithing to yourself you have just discovered the key that will unlock the door to a flow of continual financial success.

- When you come to the realization and decide with conviction that for all your hard work a part of what you earn in yours to keep, you would have found the road to increase and prosperity that can lead you on to wealth.

A Tenth Belongs To You

A tenth of what you make belongs to you, you must realize this here and now and make up your mind that you will begin to acknowledge this and appropriate this into your life.

- If you fail to do this, all you're doing is working for others and putting money in their pockets making them wealthy while your pockets go lacking.

- Until you allow this principle to work in your life, you'll never truly change your situation and circumstances. If it changes at all, it will only be a small mediocre change and nothing that will bring you to your desired financial goal.

- Until you begin to apply this principle of tithing to yourself, you will continue to pay everyone but yourself. Your labor will be only for others with nothing for yourself they will continue to increase while you continue to decrease.

Slave or Master

When you continue to pay everyone but yourself you might as well be a slave working for a master and giving him your salary as soon as your make it.

You must decide here and now whether you will continue to be a slave or become a master. Tithing to yourself accentuates the idea that you're ready to take charge of your finances.

Seed Money

The tenth that you'll keep for yourself is the seed that you will use to produce a great harvest after it's kind. Genesis 1:11-12

What small fortune would you have had if you would've taken a tenth of your salary and saved it for one year! If your salary were a minimum of $200 a week, a tenth of that would be $20 a week. In a months time that would equal out to $80 a month, and $960 a year, if your salary equals more then your tenth would be more and so will your yearly total.

That $20 is potential, it's possibility crying out to become what you want to see manifested in your financial life.

However, the past is gone but began from this day forward implementing the concept of tithing to yourself, that tenth is the starting point that makes all things feasible, performable, achievable, accessible and obtainable.

- The accumulation of the money that you will have as a result of tithing to yourself has within it the ability (**with proper knowledge**) to become the $100's, $1,000's, $10,000's, $100,000's, $1,000,000's or whatever you financially desire.

Your salary is the main object but within your salary is the tenth that belongs exclusively to you with the potential therein to bring your financial desires and thoughts to a manifest reality before your very eyes.

Within this concept of tithing to yourself live the wealth hidden that you've always longed for as you learn how to make it work for you and accumulate to an amount more than you've ever had before.

10
PAY YOUR VEHICLE

"Go to the ant, thou sluggard; consider her ways, and be wise: Which having no guide, overseer, or ruler, Provideth her meat in the summer, and gathereth her food in the harvest." Proverbs 6:6-8

Here is a concept on the road to wealth that seems strange but is an idea worth it's weight in gold. I was so impressed with this idea the first time that I heard it I immediately said to myself I must put it in one of my books for my readers.

I cannot personally take credit for this idea but I will give credit to whom it is due, a man by the name of Jesse McKay told me about the concept of paying your vehicle.

The idea of the whole thing is that if you own a vehicle of any kind eventually you're going to have to purchase something for the upkeep of that vehicle.

It matters not how new or old the vehicle is eventually the vehicle is going to require some maintenance and upkeep when such a time come the natural thing to do is either go into your account and get the money or go into your pocket to pay the expense.

Well the idea of paying your vehicle accentuates that just as you pay your bills and pay yourself you omit paying the one thing that is probably the most important material thing in your possession in this day and time, your vehicle.

We use our vehicle(s) in so many way you may not realize how important that piece of machinery is in your life, you may daily take it for granted but if you were without your vehicle for one week it would change your entire life.

I remember on an occasion I was without my vehicle for about five days and I tell you life was not the same I found out at that time the importance of having your own vehicle and keeping it up.

We Use Our Vehicle In Many Ways

- We use our vehicles to take us back and forth to work daily.

- We use our vehicles to run our errands back and forth.

- We use our vehicles to take us out of town when the need arise.

- We use our vehicles to take us places when emergencies arise.

- We use our vehicles to take us on vacations etc.

If you were to get into your vehicle right now ready to go to one of the destinations mentioned above and it refuses to start you would be shocked.

That vehicle plays a major role in our lives and we should treat it as such. The idea of paying your vehicle is a golden nugget that I chose to insert in this book that will prepare you for whatever upkeep may arise so that you will not have to take money out of your savings or pocket to pay for it.

The concept is very simple pay your vehicle just as you pay yourself, you do this by weekly putting aside a certain amount for your vehicle the amount doesn't have to be much but it must be something that you do consistently.

You can pay your vehicle ten or twenty dollars a week whatever is comfortable for you and doesn't interfere with your other expenses. You can do one of two things with the money that you pay your vehicle with you can put it in a location in your car that no one will ever find only you will know it or you can put it in an account that will give you a debit card to use for that account.

The reason for paying your vehicle is to have the money on hand at any time you need it if an emergency arise or if you need it immediately, you need to be able to get it right away.

The individual that told me about paying your vehicle related a story to me about an incident that happened once when his wife drove their vehicle out of town several hours away.

His wife telephoned him to tell him that the battery had went dead and she did not have the money on her to go and buy another battery so she needed him to wire her some money immediately.

He told her there is no need to send you any money for the car because the car has it's own money, so he told her where to go and look in the car for the money and to get out the amount for the battery and put the rest back.

Well when she went out to the car, he had about $700 that had accumulated over time in the car as a result of paying the vehicle on a continuous basis.

Readers, this concept works I use it faithfully and whenever I need anything done with my vehicle I always have the money to get it done without having to come out of my pocket or enter my savings.

You will be both surprised and thrilled if you consistently pay your vehicle for when the time arise and you have something that needs to be done all you have to do is get the vehicle money to pay for the upkeep or maintenance.

The beautiful thing also is that the amount that you consistently pay your vehicle will soon begin to accumulate into a considerable amount because you're not going to have to do upkeep weekly or monthly therefore the money will build up.

Begin to put this concept into practice and you will be glad that you did for this is just another method of discovering wealth hidden in your salary.

11
THE CYCLES OF BLESSING

"And I will restore to you the years that the locust hath eaten, the cankerworm, and the caterpillar, and the palmerworm, my great army which I sent among you. And ye shall eat in plenty, and be satisfied, and praise the name of the LORD your God, that hath dealt wondrously with you: and my people shall never be ashamed. And ye shall know that I am in the midst of Israel, and that I am the LORD your God, and none else: and my people shall never be ashamed." Joel 2:25-27

In these last days of earth's history God in his final appeal is calling the church to a higher financial calling. Through his divine providence, foresight and forethought God has made provision for and exercised infinite care over all his creation.

God is deeply touched with the cares, concerns, worries and frustrations that confront mankind on a daily basis.

God's highest wish is that *"man would prosper and be in health, even as his soul prospereth." 3 John 2* When mankind does not exemplify prosperity in every area he has fallen short of God's best for his life and has given place to the devil to buffet him.

An excellent example of an individual that had total life prosperity and had given no place to the devil to buffet him because of an open door is Job.

So the story goes, *"Now there was a day when the sons of God came to present themselves before the LORD, and Satan came also among them. And the LORD said unto Satan, Whence comest thou? Then Satan answered the LORD and said, From going to and fro in the earth, and from walking up and down in it.*

And the LORD said unto Satan, Hast thou considered my servant Job, that there is none like him in the earth, a perfect and an upright man, one that feareth God, and escheweth evil? Then Satan answered the LORD, and said, Doth Job fear God for nought?

Hast thou not made an hedge about him, and about his house, and about all that he hath on every side: thou hast blessed the work of his hands, and his substance is increased in the land." Job 1:6-10

Satan was saying to God you have given Job total life prosperity and I don't have a door to get in to buffet him through. Job was in a cycle of prosperity that few attain to in life, yet the cycle is available to all and God's highest wish for all.

The life of Job consisted of total life prosperity financially, materially, physically and spiritually. He was considered *"perfect and upright, and one that feared God, and eschewed evil."*

"And there was born unto him seven sons and three daughters. His substance also was seven thousand sheep, and three thousand camels, and five hundred she asses, and a very great household; so that this man was the greatest of all the men of the east." Job 1:1-3

Job did not get to his state of total life prosperity overnight this is one thing that we as the church have to understand. Increase is a process, prosperity is a process and wealth is a process.

- God desires to start you out first by increasing the finances that you presently have, he's not trying to make you rich at this stage, he's simply trying to increase you by entrusting you with a little bit more than you have.

- At this stage, your financial capabilities are not good in God's sight and he wants to prove you to see how you will handle a bit of increase, sad to say that most individuals fail here.

- At this stage, God wants you to learn something, he is trying to teach you that you can take that increase and begin to use it in a way that will help you to get out of your financially sick situation.

Unfortunately, most individuals fail to learn the lesson that God is trying to teach them and begin to use their increase to buy things for immediate gratification. Such things as tax returns, bonuses, rewards or unexpected monies that you receive is God's way of increasing you, however many fail here.

God in this stage is trying to teach man the principle of saving and money management. Even though a simple savings account is on the bottom totem pole of increase at least it's a start.

In the parable of the ten servants the nobleman rebuke the servant that kept laid up his pound in a napkin saying, *"thou wicked servant, Thou knewest that I was an austere man, taking up that I laid not down, and reaping that I did not sow: **Wherefore then gavest not thou my money into*** *the bank, that at my coming I might have required mine own with usury?" St. Luke 18:22-23*

In this parable, the other servants multiplied their money through trading and other business practices. However, the wicked servant refused this method of increase so the word to the wicked servant was *"if you were not going to multiply my money through trading and business practices the least you could have done is put my money into an account so that I could have gotten some interest on it."*

When God starts you out with financial increase he waits to see if you will find ways to increase your increase, spend your increase or hide your increase.

If you're of the group that will spend their increase or hide their increase, you're not ready for God to take you into prosperity or wealth.

When an individual has passed the financial increase test then God takes them from financial increase to prosperity, which is the **process** of going over and beyond your financial needs.

This is what I call the two-fold nature of prosperity one takes you beyond your needs being barely met and the other one takes you into a cycle of plenty, overflow and abundance.

A cycle is a consistent permanent and continuous pattern in ones life, events and circumstances. Cycles consist of weeks, months or years, and there's a cycle of need and there's a cycle of want.

The Cycle of Need

- The first cycle gets you in a state where you have a consistent permanent and continuous pattern of all needs met. It's a repeated flow of met needs week after week, month after month and year after year.

- When you're in this cycle of need, you have more than enough for your daily needs and you're able to do other things which individuals in poverty, lack and barely making ends meet are unable to do. There is no lack or insufficiency here you always have more than enough.

- You're a living epistle and example of 2 Corinthians 8:9 which says, *"And God is able to make all grace abound toward you: that ye always having all sufficiency in all things, may abound to every good work.*

Every saint of God can get here this is where God desires to get you first so that you can come out of financial imprisonment and lack for God isn't magnified in your lack only in your increase, prosperity and wealth.

Psalms 23:1 says, *"The LORD is my shepherd; I shall not want."* God does not want you to want for anything, God want you to be able to pay all your bills and pay them on time. God want you to have money above and beyond your bills been paid, God does not want you to want at all. The LORD is your shepherd he takes care of you and it's his job to see that your every need is supplied. It's your job to believe that he doesn't want you to want and that he is willing and able to supply your every need and give you increase.

Psalms 35:27 says, *"Let them shout for joy, and be glad, that favour my righteous cause: yea, let them say continually, Let the LORD be magnified, which hath pleasure in the prosperity of his servant."*

"The Cycle of Want"

Many times, we accept words that sound good but isn't scriptural sound. How often have your heard people say that God will supply your needs but not your wants?

Such a statement is contrary to scripture and brings forth a defeatist attitude and manner of thinking that eradicates prosperity entering your life. Anything that's not biblically sound God will not back up nor can he bless it.

When an individual say things contrary to the word of God they're taking away from scripture and making the word of God of none effect and replacing it with traditions and the words of man.

Jesus in one instance reprimanded the Pharisees and Scribes for doing this same thing saying, *"Full well ye reject the commandment of God, that ye may keep your own tradition. Making the word of God of none effect through your traditions, which ye have delivered: and many such things do ye." Mark 7:6-13*

In many instances, we find quite the contrary of these thoughts and traditions of man, throughout the scriptures we see God promising to give us what we want when we have passed the cycle of need.

1   *"Delight thyself also in the LORD, and he shall give thee the desires of thy heart."*

2   *"Let the LORD be magnified, which hath pleasure in the prosperity of his servant." Psalm 35:27b*

3   *"The righteous shall flourish like the palm tree: he shall grow like a cedar in Lebanon." Psalm 92:12*

4   *Praise ye the LORD. Blessed is the man that feareth the LORD, that delighteth greatly in his commandments. His seed shall be mighty upon earth: the generation of the upright shall be blessed. Wealth and riches shall be in his house: and his righteousness endureth for ever." Psalm 112:1-3*

5   *"That I may cause those that love me to inherit substance; and I will fill their treasures." Proverbs 8:21*

6   *"Beloved, I wish above all things that thou mayest prosper and be in health, even as thy soul prospereth." 3 John 2*

7   *"He brought them forth also with silver and gold: and there was not one feeble person among their tribes." Psalms 105:37*

The cycle of want is actually the cycle of prosperity it is a time in your life when you have gone beyond just needs been fulfilled on a continuous basis and some money left over.

- In this cycle, you have entered into a cycle of abundance, bounty and plenty. Here you are financially stable to the point where you have an overflow of finances and you're able to purchase things when you want without any financial concerns.

- You have entered into a financial realm where you're able to do more than you've ever done before. Here money comes to you easily and abundantly.

- In this cycle, you can purchase pretty much anything you want, if you need to buy something that cost you ten or twenty thousand dollars you are able to do it without any financial hurt.

You're not wealthy yet but you're financially secure and financially free from the everyday financial pressures of life that the majority of individuals go through.

It should be your objective to at least reach the cycle of want, for here is a place that others only dream of. Here you're able to freely do things with your family and friends without a financial concern in the world.

This is one of the places of promise that God has given you in his word, as the seed of Abraham

God made a promise to him that extends to you and you should lay claim upon this promise for your own life.

- According to Genesis 12:3 the word of God to Abraham was, *"And I will make of thee a great nation, and I will bless thee, and make thy name great;* **and thou shalt be a blessing**. *And I will bless them that bless thee, and curse them that curseth thee:* **and in thee shall all the families of the earth be blessed."**

God wants to bless you in such a way financially that you're able to be a financial blessing to others. However, the only way that you're truly able to be a financial blessing to others is if you're financially blessed yourself.

Sure, you can give to others when you're lacking yourself in a small way operating by the principle of sacrificial giving, but it's time to get beyond the sacrificial giving stage and come into prosperity giving.

You must come to the understanding that when God spoke to Abraham and told him *"and in thee shall all families of the earth be blessed"* you are part of the families that he was referring to. Genesis 12:3b

"Even as Abraham believed God, and it was accounted to him for righteousness. Know ye therefore that they which are of faith, the same are the children of Abraham.

And the scripture, foreseeing that God would justify the heathen through faith, preached before the gospel unto Abraham, saying, In thee shall all nations be blessed.

So then they which be of faith are blessed with faithful Abraham. And if ye be Christ's, then are ye Abraham's seed, and heirs according to the promise. Galatians 3:6-9, 29

The reason that most haven't reached the cycle of want is because even though we're heirs of God and joint-heirs with Christ position wise, yet we have not tapped into the mind of God of how to get our condition equal to our position.

Your goal is to get your condition equal to your position, you can live position wise as a Christian prosperous, rich and wealthy as an heir of God and yet die condition wise poor, broke, busted and disgusted financially and God will allow it.

The scripture says, *"Now I say, That the heir, as long as he is a child, differeth nothing from a servant, though he be lord of all."* Galatians 4:1

The second reason why God's people haven't entered the cycle of want is because we're still children and carnal in many areas.

Even though we have a right to what belongs to us, we're not able to match our position with our condition because we're still acting like children instead of grownups in our thinking and manner of life.

Paul said, *"When I was a child, I spake as a child, I understood as a child, I thought as a child: but when I became a man, I put away childish things." 1 Corinthians 13:11*

Because we continue to walk as a child, we're constantly finding our condition that of a servant though we are lord of all. As a result, Paul stated that we have to be *"under tutors and governors until the time appointed of the father."* Galatians 4:2

If we continue to walk as a child we may never enter the cycle of need and continually spend the rest of our days under the authority of others constantly finding ourselves *"the tail and not the head, the borrower instead of the lender, beneath instead of above."*

Deuteronomy 28:43-44 says it perfectly, *"The stranger that is within thee (the sinner, the world) shall get up above thee very high; and thou shalt come down very low. He shall lend to thee, and thou shalt not lend to him: he shall be the head, and thou shall be the tail."*

Yet, when we learn to walk as mature Christians then God shall reverse the condition and make us the head and not the tail, the lender and not the borrower, above only and never beneath, if we obey his word and apply the things you're learning in this book.

Our position is a settled and fixed position, we're already positioned for increase, prosperity and wealth just by being a son of God. Our position cannot be anymore than it already is you're right now a son of the living God.

At this present moment as a born again believer *"All things are yours; Whether Paul, or Apollos, or Cephas, or the world, or life, or death, or things present, or things to come; all are yours; and ye are Christ's; and Christ is God's"* 1 Corinthians 3:21-23

It's time to enter the cycle of want and begin to live the prosperous life that is rightly yours as a son of God, stop believing the reports of the enemy and of those that tell you God will not give you what you want.

Look at their life, are they where you want to be then they have no right to instruct you about where you can attain to, in their own mind they are wise yet they desire to have more than they have.

In God's eyes, they are sluggards and he has many things to say about sluggards, and none of it is good.

- *"The sluggard is wiser in his own conceit than seven men that can render a reason." Proverbs 26:16*

- *"Go to the ant, thou sluggard; consider her ways, and be wise: Which having no guide, overseer, or ruler, Provideth her meat in the summer, and gathereth her food in the harvest. How long wilt thou sleep, O sluggard? when wilt thou arise out of thy sleep? Yet a little sleep, a little slumber, a little folding of the hands to sleep. So shall thy poverty come as one that travelleth, and thy want as an armed man." Proverbs 6:6-11*

- *The soul of the sluggard desireth, and hath nothing: but the soul of the diligent shall be made fat." Proverbs 13:4*

- *The sluggard shall not plow by reason of*

*the cold; therefore shall he beg in harvest,
and have nothing." Proverbs 20:4*

God wants you to increase, prosper and have abundance therefore you should obey God rather than man the scriptures are plain you need not add anything to it nor take anything away.

God's thoughts toward you are, *"Beloved, I wish above all things that thou mayest prosper and be in health, even as thy soul prospereth." 3 John 2*

12
THE CYCLE OF WEALTH

"But thou shalt remember the LORD thy God: for it is he that giveth thee power to get wealth, that he may establish his covenant which he sware unto thy fathers, as it is this day." Deuteronomy 8:18

We have just looked at the cycle of need and the cycle of want, the first is a condition that God blesses us to get to where we're no longer struggling financially, all our needs are met with some left over to enjoy life. The second cycle is a condition that God has blessed you to arrive where you're living financially in abundance, plenty and overflow, here you have more than enough to do whatever you need to do without any financial concerns.

Now we arrive to the ultimate financial condition the cycle of wealth. If you don't believe that God wants you here then you will never get here, the cycle of wealth belongs to you just as much as the cycle of need and want.

In the cycle of wealth this is the process of accumulating riches your condition is one of immense wealth you're a millionaire to say the least but more likely a multi-millionaire.

- In this cycle, money is no object to you for you have more than enough for life necessities and cares. Financially you're one to be reckoned with God has blessed you in such a way that your fame has spread abroad. *"The blessing of the LORD, it maketh rich, and he addeth no sorrow with it." Proverbs 10:22*

- In this cycle, God has blessed you to amass such a fortune that your wealth opens doors for you and brings you before great men, people gives you things simply because you're rich. *"The rich hath many friends." Proverbs 10:20b*

- In this cycle, people are clamoring for your attention because they want to know what you know and how to get where God has blessed you to arrive. When you get here you're news and both the world and the saints desire to be around you because they're curious about how you've become rich and wealthy.

Throughout the scriptures we see many that has entered the cycle of wealth and their lifestyle display one of plenty and abundance. Many times individuals will speak against the wealthy for having an abundance of material things not realizing that such individuals can't help but have much stuff because they have so much money.

In biblical times we see the example of a man of God by the name of Job, we've looked at Job already but now let's observe him in another light. This man Job had entered the cycle of wealth, his story reads like the lifestyle of the rich and famous.

"There was a man in the land of Uz, whose name was Job; and that man was perfect and upright, and one that feared God and eschewed evil. And there was born unto him seven sons and three daughters.

His substance also was seven thousand sheep, and three thousand camels, and five hundred yoke of oxen, and five hundred she asses, and a very great household; **so that this man was the greatest of all the men of the east.***" Job 1:1-3*

Job had entered a place of wealth where only one percent of the world reaches, however there is no stipulation that emphasizes only one percent of the world can attain this.

Anyone that can believe God and willing to pay the price and have a strong enough desire and determination with appropriate plans can be in that one percent. Proverbs 10:4

Individuals from all walks of life have arrived here from farmers, school dropouts and individuals that lived in bad conditions etc. have entered the cycle of wealth.

What you must realize is that wealth and riches come from God when the sinner man or saint attain the cycle of wealth in a legal way God was the chief cause of man accumulating his wealth. God is the source of wealth.

If man refuse to give God credit for his wealth we still know that man did not wake himself up everyday to go forth in his occupation to accumulate his wealth, God woke him up and strengthen him for his daily task.

In the book of Chronicles David speaks forth praises of thanksgiving to God as he acknowledge him as the possessor of all things saying, *"Thine, O LORD is the greatness, and the power, and the glory, and the victory, and the majesty: for all that is in the heaven and in the earth is thine; thine is the kingdom, O LORD, and thou art exalted as head above all.*

Both riches and honour come of thee, and thou reignest over all; and in thine hand is power and might; and in thine hand it is to make great, and to give strength unto all. Now therefore, our God, we thank thee, and praise thy glorious name." 1 Chronicles 29:11-13

The cycle of wealth is a glorious condition to be in for with wealth there are so many good things you can do, the scriptures say, *"When the righteous are in authority, the people rejoice: but when the wicked beareth rule, the people mourn."*

When you're living in a city and you're wealthy, God uses you to cause that city to rejoice. If you're a businessperson and a millionaire, you can employ at least ten people in your business making jobs available. If you're a billionaire, you can employ thousands of people thereby making multitudes of jobs available.

In either condition, you have just caused ten or thousands of people to rejoice in the city you live in because of your financial status. When wealth is in the hands of the righteous exploits can be done for the glory of God and the good of man.

- Having wealth will enable you to be able to help spread the gospel to the ends of the earth.

- Having wealth will enable you to help support missionaries and pay for radio and television time for your personal ministry or other ministries that has the call of God on their life.

- Having wealth will enable you to help pay for the publication of Christian literature and books.

- Having wealth will enable you to feed the poor, clothe the naked and provide housing and transportation for those lest fortunate.

- Having wealth will enable you to build Christian schools and places of education for the whole man, it will enable you to have business schools and financial classes that will help individuals learn financial matters and become financially competent.

This cycle of wealth is a good thing and a condition attainable by anyone that desires to attain it with all things being equal.

In the scriptures we see another of God's servants that had entered the cycle of wealth and became very rich, in Genesis 13:2 it says, *"And Abram was very rich in cattle, in silver, and in gold. And Lot also, which went with Abram, had flocks, and herds, and tents. And the land was not able to bear them, that they might dwell together: for their substance was great, so that they could not dwell together.*"

What a condition to be in, having so much wealth and possessions that you and your brother or sister in Christ can't live beside each other because your substance has become too great.

Remember saints of God we're serving the same God yesterday, today and forever and we're serving him under a better covenant with better promises. *"But now hath he obtained a more excellent ministry, by how much also he is the mediator of a better covenant, which was established upon better promises." Hebrews 8:6*

And what shall I more say, for the time would fail me to tell of other wealthy saints of God throughout the scriptures like, *"Isaac, Jacob, Joseph, Moses, the children of Israel, Joshua, the Judges, the Kings, David, Solomon, the Apostles: who lived in the cycle of wealth and contributed greatly to the cause of God in the earth.*

Now it's your time dear saint to come into the cycle of wealth, God wants you there it's his good pleasure to give you the kingdom

"Every man also to whom God hath given riches and wealth, and hath given him power to eat

thereof, and to take his portion, and to rejoice in his labour; this is the gift of God." Ecclesiastes 5:19

"A feast is made for laughter, and wine maketh merry: but money answereth all things." Ecclesiastes 10:19

"Moreover the profit of the earth is for all: the king himself is served by the field." Ecclesiastes 5:9

"For wisdom is a defence and money is a defence." Ecclesiastes 7:12a

"For ye know the grace of our Lord Jesus Christ, that, though he was rich, yet for your sakes he became poor, that ye through his poverty might be rich." 2 Corinthians 8:9

The cycle of wealth belongs to you, you can have it if you can believe it and receive it.

13
CONDITION MATCHES
POSITION

This is probably the most difficult chapter to write because this chapter has to have information that is applicable to show you how to get your condition to match your position.

It must show you how to get from where you are to where you should be in the financial and material arena of your life. Presently you may be living in a state of poverty, lack, barely making ends meet or paycheck living.

My job as the author is to give you principles and answers that will show you how to get from where you are to where you want to be.

1   Two things are important at this stage to take you from where you are to where you should be there is nothing new under the

sun so I'm not giving you any new information.

2   Any information that you learn here is either lost information, information that you've never heard before or information that you've never heard in this manner.

First, you cannot go any further than what you know, you're limited by the knowledge that you have or by the knowledge that you have but aren't applying. In the book of Hosea it says, *"My people are destroyed for lack of knowledge: because thou hast rejected knowledge, I will also reject thee."* Hosea 4:6

One bit of knowledge that's vital to get you from where you are to where you want to be is *"you must know what you want in life, you must have a definite purpose."* If you don't know what you want in life how will you ever attain it, how will you have what you don't know you want?

Until you get this bit of knowledge answered, you'll never be able to go much further in life. Right now what is it that you want in life financially and materially to just say plenty of money is to vague, it has no life in it and therefore you have no unction to go after it.
Right now, say a financial goal that you desire to have in your life that you're willing to pay the price to attain even if it makes you shame. Forget

about whether you can achieve it just say it.

Now that you've said it you know what you want financially in life, I have good news for you whatever financial amount you said somebody has already attained it in life.

What one man or woman can do another man or woman can do. History, success magazines, books and the bible itself are filled with men and women that has already gone before you and achieved that amount in life.

I'm almost one hundred percent sure, that nobody in their financial statement affirmed the amount of fifty billion dollars well even this amount has been attained by some.

Therefore, your spoken statement is definitely possible and attainable with the proper knowledge.

Second, you must have a vision of what it is you want to attain in life for "*without a vision the people perish.*" Proverbs 29:18 A vision can be termed as a goal or an objective having this gives you something to strive for something to work towards.

With a goal or objective in mind you have something before you to work towards without a

104

goal or objective you have nothing to pursue or go after. Goal isn't a bad word it's just a term stating your objective or desire, however if you would like a more sophisticated term you can use **"Prosperity Target."**

That which you spoke out as a financial attainment, is your prosperity target that's what you're shooting for and the good news is that God wants you to have it. In Jeremiah it says, *"For I know the thoughts that I think toward you, saith the LORD, thoughts of peace (**prosperity, wellness, health, safety, blessing, happiness and plenty**), and not thoughts of evil (**grief, calamity, sorrow, trouble, and affliction**), to give you an expected end (**a future, a hope and success**)."* Jeremiah 29:11

Now that you have a prosperity target, next you must have a plan for increase. A strategy to get you there and the good news is that there's not just one strategy to get you there, there are many strategies that can get you there.

A strategy is nothing more than a plan an approach a tactic and a line of attack, daily you have strategies that you accomplish, some have become such a part of your everyday routine that you no longer see it as a strategy.

1   Here is an elementary example, at one time and point you had to make a plan or method of how to do what you easily do today without effort. A simple point in case is the place that you currently live, when you first moved there you had to come up with an approach or strategy of how to easily get there without taking a longer route.

2   You may have tried two different ways but finally settled on a certain way as the easiest way to get there, all you did was looked at both ways and then settled on the way that you thought was best. Now, the way that you take you take it effortlessly because your strategy is already in place.

When you take a trip or vacation to a specific place, you don't just jump up and go you plan and strategize the whole trip from beginning to end.

Well if you're planning everyday of your life anyway and you plan your vacations and trips why can't you plan how to attain your prosperity target? Strategizing how to reach your prosperity target is no harder than planning for your next vacation, when you know where you want to go then you begin to call around and get the appropriate information needed to get you there.

Likewise, when you want to reach your prosperity target you must get the appropriate knowledge needed to show you how to get there. This knowledge is available in books, tapes, seminars etc., it's there for your learning and you must go forth after it.

Your plan for increase includes all or some of these methods to get you from where you are to where you want to be. Somebody knows how to get you there for somebody has gone where you desire to be, no need to reinvent the wheel just talk to the man that invented it.

- You talk to the man by reading his books listening to his tapes going to his seminars and then applying what you learn. As Christians, we've become so spiritual that we believe that God will tell us everything to do, this isn't so if it were then God would not have blessed men and women with the gift of writing, the gift of teaching and given us all these modern days inventions of learning.

- **Use what's out there, it's not sinful to read a book by a man that's telling you how to be financially free and he's not a Christian, this man obviously have**

tapped into something that has caused him to increase, prosper or become financially wealthy.

• Take the time to learn what this person has learned whether they are saint or sinner as long as they're telling you truth that is legal and you're able to apply it.

Throughout the scriptures, we have an abundance of word that accentuates to us the importance of learning, counsel and acquiring knowledge. As saints of God, we haven't yet learned the importance of increasing our learning the world has learned it and applies it faithfully.

The scriptures say, **"The children of this world are in their generation wiser than the children of light." Luke 16:8**

The word of God consistently tells us about learning saying, *"A wise man will hear, and will increase learning; and a man of understanding shall attain unto wise counsels." Proverbs 1:5*

"Yea, if thou criest after knowledge, and liftest up thy voice for understanding; If thou seekest her as silver, and searchest for her as for hid treasures; Then shalt thou understand the fear of the LORD, and find the knowledge of God." Proverbs 2:3-5

"Hear instructions, and be wise, and refuse it not. Blessed is the man that heareth me, watching daily at my gates, waiting at the posts of my doors. For whoso findeth me findeth life, and shall obtain favour of the LORD." Proverbs 8:33-35

"Give instruction to a wise man, and he will be yet wiser: teach a just man, and he will increase in learning." Proverbs 9:9

"Without counsel purposes are disappointed; but in the multitude of counselors they are established." Proverbs 15:22

"Every purpose is established by counsel: and with good advice make war." Proverbs 20:18

The learning and instructions that you need to get you from where you are to where you want to be is written in some book some where, is being taught right now at some seminar, is being lectured in some classroom, has being recorded on a tape, video or CD, somebody already knows what you want to know.

God is not going to tell you everything you have to go forth and seek out knowledge seek out the information that you need that will cause you to increase, prosper and acquire wealth. Matthew 7:7-8

Knowledge is power and the more of it you have the more power you have and the more you're able to do. Little knowledge equals little power, much knowledge equals much power and an abundance of knowledge equals an abundance of power.

"Wise man lay up knowledge: but the mouth of the foolish is near destruction." Proverbs 10:14

"Whoso loveth instruction loveth knowledge: but he that hateth reproof is brutish." Proverbs 12:1

"Also, that the soul be without knowledge, it is not good." Proverbs 19:2

From this day forward, make it your business to get the necessary knowledge that you need to help you get ahead in the game of life. Knowledge is available everywhere you turn it's dispersed abroad and waiting for you to come after it.

Do whatever you have to do to get your condition equivalent to your position, go back to school, take up a home-study course, a course on the internet, buy the necessary books, tapes, video, CD that you need, **just do something and do it now.**

This might seem elementary to say but stop waiting around for some great move of God upon your life to tell you go better your life, common sense tells you to better your life so that you can come out of your financial sick situation.

1 Shake yourself loose from that **spirit of indecision** that hounds you daily to the point where you want take that class you need to further yourself.

2 Shake yourself loose from that **spirit of slothfulness** that slows you down from going forward to attain that which you financially desire in life.

3 Shake yourself loose from that **spirit of procrastination** that causes you to keep putting off doing what you know you need to do to see a change in your financial life.

4 Shake yourself loose from that **spirit of laziness** that makes you lethargy, sluggish and idle to the point that you have no get up and go about you to attain that which you desire.

In the name of Jesus Christ bind that spirit and command it to go from your life so that you can be about your father's business and accomplish the things he has destined for your life.

From this day forward let your daily word be **action** for it's action that gets things done, knowledge alone will not get it, action needs to be applied to the knowledge that you learn.

"Even so faith, if it hath not works (action), is dead, being alone. Yea, a man may say, Thou hast faith, and I have works: shew me thy faith without they works, and I will shew thee my faith by my works.

But wilt thou know, O vain man, that faith without works (action) is dead, being alone. For as the body without the spirit is dead, so faith without works is dead also." James 2:14-26

So let us hear the conclusion of the whole matter of getting your condition to meet your position:

- You can go no further than what you know therefore you must acquire knowledge.

- You must know what you want in life.

- Say a financial goal that you desire to have in life aloud right now.

- You must have a vision and objective to strive for you must have a prosperity target to shoot for.

- God's thoughts toward you, is peace not evil to give you an expected end.

- You must have a strategy, a plan, an approach, a tactic, or a line of attack to get you from where you are to where you want to be.

- You must learn from others who have gone where you desire to be.

- Read their books, listen to their tapes, videos, CD's etc.

- JUST DO SOMETHING AND DO IT NOW!

- Shake yourself loose from indecision, slothfulness, procrastination and laziness.

- Let your daily word be ACTION!

Doing these things will assist you in getting your condition equivalent to your position, not to have your condition equivalent to your position is to settle for life's crumbs when you could have had the whole cake.

14
THE SPIRIT OF POVERTY

Financial prosperity is a subject that I love to talk about because it's God's highest wish that his people prosper. In 3 John 2 it says, *"Beloved, I wish above all things that thou mayest prosper and be in health, even as thy soul prospereth."*

However, many of God's people are living more in poverty than in prosperity, sure there are some saints prospering but the majority are barely making ends meet.

There are several reasons for poverty I will list three in particular:

1 The first reason is sin, the second is man's own laziness and slothfulness the third is a spirit of poverty.

2 The first came as a result of the fall, the second is a result of man's unwillingness to take the initiative to act and do in order to prosper.

3   The third is a spirit whose focus is to bind mankind in the area of finances this spirit's main focus is to keep you in lack, limitation and barely making ends meet no matter how much you work.

If it seems as though no matter what you do you still aren't able to get a breakthrough financially maybe you're in bondage by a spirit of poverty.

In the gospel of Luke Jesus loosed a woman that was bound by a spirit of infirmity, even though she was a daughter of Abraham and had rights according to the covenant she was yet in bondage by this spirit.

Jesus stated, *"And ought not this woman, being a daughter of Abraham, whom Satan hath bound, lo, these eighteen years, be loosed from this bond on the Sabbath day?" Luke 13:10-16*

Maybe you've been bound for many years by this spirit of poverty while yet being the seed of Abraham and heirs according to the promise. You should be loosed now from this bond. Galatians 3:29

Until that spirit of poverty is broken over your life, it could hinder the manifestation of your confession from coming forth. This is the problem of many, that spirit must be broken so that you can be loosed from this bond so that the fullness of your blessings can come forth.

Let's pray this prayer right now so that the spirit of poverty can be broken over your life. Pray it with boldness and authority.

"Father I thank you that those which the Son set free are free indeed. In the name of Jesus Christ, I command this spirit of poverty to be broken over my life now. I bind it on earth Father as you bound it in heaven. I command you spirit of poverty to go forth from me and never return in the name of Jesus Christ. I now loose the abundance and Divine supply of God to be manifest for me now in rich appropriate form. God is now opening the way for my immediate blessings and I receive it now, financial increase, prosperity and wealth shall be manifested in my life for I am an heir of God and joint-heir with Jesus Christ I am the seed of Abraham and have a right to increase, prosperity and wealth. In Jesus Name, I receive it now, Amen.

Financial Prosperity Affirmations

Financial prosperity belongs to you everyday you're surrounded with an abundance of things everything that you could possibly wish for has been placed within your easy reach.

God certainly intended that everyone that wishes for an abundance and is willing to work for an abundance should have an abundance for in life there is enough and to spare.

God desires that you prosper Jesus died to deliver you from the curse of poverty. Poverty was not God's original intention for man, God established a covenant saying, *"But thou shalt remember the LORD thy God: for it is he that giveth thee power to get wealth, that he may establish his covenant which he sware unto thy fathers as it is this day."* *Deuteronomy 8:18*

Financial freedom can be yours many individuals started right where you are some in worse situations yet they rose above their circumstances to fulfill their financial dream.

Your financial destiny is within your hands affirming or confessing your financial prosperity starts you out right.

FINANCIAL PROSPERITY AFFIRMATIONS

1   *"It is God that gives me power to get wealth, that he may establish his covenant which he sware unto the fathers, as it is this day. I am getting wealthier everyday."* *Deuteronomy 8:18*

2   *"Prosperity is working right now and continually finding ways to come into my life."*

3   *"The LORD is my shepherd I shall not want, all my bills are paid in full now." Psalms 23:1*

4   *"But my God shall supply all my need, according to his riches in glory by Christ Jesus." Philippians 4:19*

5   *Money loves to fill my pockets therefore my pockets are filled with money now.*

6   *Money comes to me easily and abundantly I am blessed going and coming. Deuteronomy 28*

7   *"Wealth and riches are in my house." Psalms 112:3*

8   *"I am the head and not the tail I am above only and never beneath I am the lender and not the borrower, I am blessed of God." Deuteronomy 28*

9   *God is the creator of the universe he is both rich and wealthy and he is now showing me how to claim my own God given wealth. He is now moving on my*

behalf and opening the way for my immediate blessings.

FINANCIAL PROSPERITY CONFESSION TARGET

When you are in pursuit of something it makes sense to have an objective or goal at which to aim for, in this case you have your prosperity target.

Your goal is for you and not to be measured by anyone else's goal. Your prosperity target is what you will shoot for and what you shall attain to, now what we will do is give you a formula for confessing your target in an orderly manner that will cover your financial goal and cause you to boldly confess it outwardly.

As you get started confessing your prosperity target, realize that your confessions are a powerful means for conditioning and renewing your mind so that you can perform in every area of your life with an optimist attitude. Romans 12:1-2

Next to building up your spirit, nothing is more important than a healthy state of mind. As your mind is renewed, it in turn affects your spirit and you become strong in both mind and spirit.

A healthy and strong mind and spirit conditions you for life situations and then nothing shall be impossible unto you. Mark 11:22-24

GUIDELINES FOR AFFIRMING CONFESSIONS

Always confess that something is happening here and now do not confess that something will happen in the future or that something is going to happen.

Such confessions are actually negative confessions, which says "Someday I will be wealthy or I am going to be wealthy." Place the results in today let it be now, "*Now faith is*." Hebrews 11:1

One thing I want to bear hard in mind in this section is that even though some confessions happen immediately the majority of them do not happen overnight.

Here's something that you need to understand about confession, the moment you begin to confess a thing that thing begins to draw toward you from the time that you begin confessing until the time the confession is manifested before your very eyes.

The more you confess a thing the closer the thing gets to you that you're confessing, when you start out you may not have full faith that the thing you're confessing shall happen, but cast that thought aside and know that your confession is drawing the thing to you at every confession.

Understand that it want happen just because you say it once or twice but the moment you really get that thing in your spirit and believe it your confession at that point is a reality.

At that moment it has become just as real to you as if you already have in your possession the thing you've confessed. When your confession has gotten into your spirit, it's alive and active and your belief is a thousand times stronger than any belief you can have in your mind alone.

When your confession has found a home in your spirit then it has become a part of you, then you shall have that which you've confessed and nothing shall be impossible unto you.

Confession Plus Action
Equals Financial Success

As you do your confession on a daily basis there are several ways that God will bring your confession to pass. In one instance you may begin to notice that you have **hunches** or

inspirations that comes to you to do certain things that will cause that which you've confess to come to pass.

Another method that God may use is by means of other individuals, he may have an individual to tell you something that you need to know that's the answer to what you've been confessing.
Or he may use a person to give you that which you've been confessing. In many cases of confession individuals have simply come to the one doing the confessing and given them money, clothes etc.

The individual doing the giving may not necessarily know they're the instrument that God is using to bring your confession to pass only God and your family member will know about your confession for you're doing it in secret, but God will reward you openly. Matthew 6:4

God can use a number of methods to bring your confession to pass he is God and he has all the answers and methods that's needed to make it happen.

If God uses the method of hunches or inspiration by speaking to your spirit about something to do or say, don't be slothful put it into action immediately. Proverbs 12:24, 27, 15:19, 18:9, 19:15,24, 21:25, 22:13

The thing to remember is whatever way God chooses you must take action for therein lives your breakthrough. If you do not take action then all your confessing would have been nothing more than a chasing of the wind, you are confessing something that you desire to see happen in your life now let it happen.

Your confession shall come true it's your job to recognize God's method and move when God move and always give him praise for the answer, for therein lies your destiny your answer and God's manifestation of your confession.

The key word is action make that move, act now and receive your confession, do your confession at least twice daily, morning and night before you go to sleep. James 2:26

FINANCIAL PROSPERITY CONFESSION

(Here write your financial prosperity target)

Confess: I am a very prosperous person, I _____(say your name)
Now have in my possession _____(say your financial prosperity target) which have come to me from time to time and all at once.

Money have come to me from many sources the divine supply of God has brought substance of increase, prosperity and wealth to me now.

*I have this money in my possession now, I now see it before my eyes (**actually see yourself in possession of the money**) I now touch it with my hands, it is now transferred to me because I have given of my tithes and offerings and confessed it in return for it.*

God has opened up the windows of heaven for me now, fresh ideas, new understanding, knowledge and wisdom I now receive.

The Holy Spirit has directed abundance to me from God's riches in glory by Christ Jesus. The wealth of the sinner is given to me now, financial increase and prosperity is in my possession.

I am blessed of God, I am blessed going and coming, I am the head and not the tail, I am above only and never beneath, I am the lender and not the borrower. Hallelujah, I am financially blessed and prosperous. I have received my prosperity target of _____ money loves to be in my possession.

15

Use Your Salary for Increase, Prosperity and Wealth

"Moreover the profit of the earth is for all: the king himself is served by the field. A man's gift maketh room for him and bringeth him before great men." Ecclesiastes 5:9, Proverbs 18:16

If one individual can have financial increase, prosperity and wealth so can you there's no ifs, and or buts about it what one person can do another can do.

Up to this point, you've learned many things about discovering wealth hidden in your salary now it's time to do something with what you know.

Let's do a summary of the things you've learned so far in the former chapters:

- *POTENTIAL, here you learned that potential is present but not visible or active power, it's power that lies dormant or inactive, yet within that inactive power lies the ability to make things happen or bring things to pass.*

- *DIVINE HELP IN GETTING YOUR WEALTH, here you learned that God has given his angels charge over your life and they are assigned to help you in life and could be the missing link in helping you to get your wealth.*

- *THE POWER TO THINK, here you learned that one of the most important and overlooked things are the thoughts that you allow to dominate your thinking for we become what we think about.*

- *SALARY, here you learned that salary is defined as wages that one receives for his or her services it is payment for work rendered. Also, we accepted salary as any legal kind of income that you have coming to you on a weekly, bi-weekly or monthly basis.*

- *YOU MUST DO SOMETHING DIFFERENT, here you've discovered that if you want something that you've never had then you must do something that you've never done. If you keep repeating the same process, you're going to keep getting the same results you can't expect different results following the same pattern.* ,

- **THE TITHES**, *here you learned that this is the one main obedient call that God is making to his people, a call to return to him in bringing their tithes and offering to the house of God. Nothing else that we do will make up for our neglect in bringing the tithes.*

- **TRUSTING GOD**, *here you learned that in order to operate in God's plan of economy we must come to the conclusion that God is our source. We must learn to trust God with what we have or else we'll never see the mighty works of God in our behalf.*

- **THE POWER OF GIVING**, *here we've learned that many times in life, we greatly desire to receive but the key to receiving is understanding that, "it's more blessed to give than to receive." Acts 20:35*

- **TITHE TO YOURSELF**, *this is the principle of taking a portion of the money that you make and pay yourself just as* *faithful as you pay your bills or bring your tithes to the house of God. Here you will take out ten percent (no less than five percent) of your income and setting it aside to build your wealth.*

- **PAY YOUR VEHICLE,** *here you learned that your vehicle is one of the most important material things you possess and you should pay it weekly or monthly just like you pay your bills and yourself.*

- **THE CYCLE OF BLESSING,** *here you learned that in life there are cycles which man operates by whether he realize it or not your objective is to get into the cycle of need and then go further into the cycle of want.*

- **THE CYCLE OF WEALTH,** *this is the cycle that accentuates the process of accumulating riches here your condition is one of immense wealth you're a millionaire to say the least but more likely a multi-millionaire.*

- **CONDITION MATCHES POSITION,** *here you learned that as a child of God, your position is already one of increase, prosperity and wealth, but you must get your condition to match your position.*

- ***THE SPIRIT OF POVERTY, here you learned that there is a spirit whose main focus is to bind mankind in the area of their finances, this spirit's main focus is to keep you in lack, limitation and barely making ends meet no matter how much you work.***

Now in this chapter it's time to take action and apply what you learned to your every day life. Do not allow another day to pass if you haven't begin to put into action the things you've learned in this book, otherwise you have knowledge but no action.

Every chapter is vital toward your financial success but the chapter I want to focus on that will enable you to start your financial portfolio increasing is the chapter ***"TITHE TO YOURSELF."***

This chapter emphasizes the importance of putting aside ten percent (*no less than five percent*) of your income for yourself, this tithe to yourself is your seed money this is money that will produce for you your harvest.

Let's reiterate here: What small fortune would you have had if you would've taken a tenth of your salary and saved it for a year? If your salary were a minimum of $200 a week, a tenth of that would be $20 a week. In a month's time that would be $80 a month, in a year's time that equals $960.00, if your income is more then your weekly, monthly and yearly tithe to yourself will be more.

Here as I've always been I'm going to be frank and blunt with you because I want you to know the whole truth and the truth will set you free others may not tell you this but I will because I have nothing to lose and I want you prosper.

The truth is you can bring your tithes and offering into the house of God plant financial seeds and still die in poverty barely making ends meet and living paycheck to paycheck.

In order to increase you must have more than just spiritual knowledge you must also have financial knowledge about how to make your finances work once God has blessed you to increase.

The majority of Christians know nothing about how to make their finances work for them instead of against them. Once you have money that money is to be used to make more money not to go and spend on things right away, if you can hold off on the things for just a little while and let your money work for you, after awhile you'll be able to buy those things and pay cash money.

Repeat this with me: "My concept of money is to let my money that I've accumulated make more money for me." Repeat it again.

Here I will accentuate ideas that I've written in a prior book about how to have financial increase, prosperity and wealth, truth remains the same it does not change if you didn't apply these avenues for prosperity before now is the time. (*See our book "Hidden Riches of Secret Places"*)

The money that you've saved in paying yourself is the money that you will use for financial increase, prosperity and wealth.

CHOOSE YOUR AVENUE FOR PROSPERITY

Depending on the type of prosperity that you desire you will have to choose the avenue that can produce for you that type of increase, prosperity and wealth. It's very unlikely that you're going to become a millionaire working a 9-5 job.

Every cycle that you enter you must first enter it in your imagination in the time of your mediation you must act as if you're already there, see yourself doing what you would do when you physically enter that cycle. (*See our book "Hidden Riches of Secret Places" and "Faith*

131

Will Prosper You Everytime.")

On a job, your prosperity is limited to a certain amount, however, with wise management a little can become a lot.

At this time, we will name four different avenues for increase, prosperity and wealth, as you choose the avenue that best suits you continually think about the flow of money and wealth.

Get into an avenue of prosperity whereby money flows near you in order to stimulate your interest about money and how it turns over profits. **The best choice out of the four avenues is the one that best fits your gifts and talents, don't choose an avenue just for money sakes but choose the one that you will derive the most pleasure in doing.**

These avenues makes the difference between the individual that just do the spiritual things with their money such as bringing the tithes, offering and planting seeds verses the ones that does the spiritual things plus applies their money to one or more of these four avenues. Most Christians just set back and wait for God to do some miraculous financial miracle to improve their finances, well if he does grant you a financial miracle if you don't use one or more of these four avenues to keep that increase flowing you're going to be right back where you started. Use what you have and apply what you've learned in this book and behold all things are yours.

FOUR AVENUES TO WEALTH

* **First, there is the avenue of Business-**This is one of the fastest ways to get prosperity rushing to you. In business, you must have some type of product or service that you can offer clients in return for money. All of the large companies today started out with one or two products today they are million and billion dollar corporations. Every business has the potential to take you into increase, prosperity and wealth. Some business can be started with as little as a hundred dollars some may take a couple of thousands but with the proper knowledge, determination, a definite plan and a burning desire you can succeed.

The business that you have in mind somebody somewhere is prospering doing it or something similar, remember what one individual can do another can do. **Put action behind the tithe to yourself money and learn what it takes to succeed in that business and go forth and obtain your increase, prosperity and wealth in business**.

If you need ideas and more information concerning various businesses ideas we will be more than happy to direct you to the pertinent information that will assist you with different money making ideas. Just email us at **millions737@yahoo.com** and in the subject area put **Business Ideas Information** or go to our website **www.dexterjonesministries.org** and under **Free Information** click on **Business Ideas.**

Second, there is the avenue of Investing-This is another avenue that can produce increase, prosperity and wealth for you when used with financial literacy and competency. There are many types of investments options such as stocks, bonds, mutual funds etc. there are conservative investments, moderately aggressive investments and very aggressive investments. Investments can be started with different amounts depending on the type of investment that you would like to invest in. There are many books, seminars and investment managers that can start you on the right road to investing. Check out the many sources that are available to you, talk with individuals that you know who are already investing and read good books on investing. Many individuals have become millionaires and billionaires through investing. The investment world is another profitable avenue for increase, prosperity and wealth.

134

If you need additional information on investing we will be more than happy to direct you to the appropriate information that will assist you in becoming an investor and learn how to use proven strategies and make money consistently. This information is vital if you want to win in the avenue of investing. Just email us at **millions737@yahoo.com** and in the subject area put **Investing Information** or go to our website **www.dexterjonesministries.org** and under **Free Information** click on **Investing.**

- **Third, there is the avenue of Real Estate-** This is one avenue that many years ago experience a great real estate boom, and many millionaires were produced. Real estate is still a very lucrative business and avenue for increase, prosperity and wealth. There are many mentors that you can learn from that can put you on the right track for financial success in this area. Likewise, there are seminars you can attend, books you can read and a variety of information available to you. The real estate world is another avenue for increase, prosperity and wealth,

If you need additional information on how to get into Real Estate we have the answers for you we can direct you to the most important information you will need to know in order to make it big in

Real Estate. If you want to win in this lucrative business just email us at **millions737@yahoo.com** and in the subject area put **Real Estate Information** or go to our website **ww.dexterjonesministries.org** and under **Free Information** click on **Real Estate.**

- **Fourth, there is the avenue of the Internet-**This is an avenue that can literally produce increase, prosperity and wealth for anybody. Nothing equals the internet's potential this is the information super highway and it offers possibilities and potential to make money like nothing the world has ever seen. With the right information and know-how, you can literally become rich working from the privacy of your own home. The most attractive product to sell over the Internet is information however any product that meets a need is a good sell with the right customer base. The Internet world is a very profitable and lucrative avenue that can produce for you increase, prosperity and wealth. Learn from those that have already succeeded in this area.If you need additional information concerning how to make money on the internet we have the information for you. We can direct you to the appropriate information that can show you how to make money with your computer. Your computer can become your own personal cash register a continuous money machine. Just email us at **millions737@yahoo.com** and in the subject area put **Internet Information** or go to our website **www.dexterjonesministries. org** and under **Free Information** click on **Internet Cash Register.**

If there is any additional information you may need just email us with your questions and we will direct you to the most pertinent information that's sure to assist you in **Discovering Wealth.**

Now you know the reason that I strongly emphasized tithing to yourself for that money is the seed that you will use to produce your harvest. The majority of individuals today are continually eating their seeds and therefore they have nothing to plant toward bringing their dreams to pass.

Well the truth is it's going to take money to bring your dreams to pass and the money is already hidden in your salary and now through the knowledge you've received in this book you know that it's there and how to use it to attain your prosperity target, therefore just do it and increase, prosperity and wealth will come to you as sure as the night follows the day.

16
Financial Freedom

"I made me great works; I builded me houses; I planted me vineyards: I made me gardens and orchards, and I planted trees in them of all kind of fruits: I made me pools of water, to water therewith the wood that bringeth forth trees: I got me servants and maidens, and had servants born in my house; also I had great possessions of great and small cattle above all that were in Jerusalem before me: I gathered me also silver and gold, and the peculiar treasure of kings and of the provinces: I gat me men singers and women singers, and the delights of the sons of men, as musical instruments, and that of all sorts. So I was great, and increased more than all that were before me in Jerusalem: also my wisdom remained with me." Ecclesiastes 2:4-9

Financial freedom what beautiful words to voice it's indeed a blessing when an individual can say that God has blessed me to be financially free. Financial freedom is God's desire for everyone of his children God is greatly concerned with increase, prosperity and wealth in your life he wants you to have it.

Throughout the scriptures we see the word increase accentuated in different instances, in the New Testament the word is mentioned nine times eight of those times God is promoting enlargement, to raise, add to, multiply and enhancement. Luke 17:5, John 3:30, 1 Corinthians 3:6, 1 Corinthians 3:7, 2 Corinthians 9:10, Ephesians 4:16, 1 Thessalonians 3:12, 4:10,

In the Old Testament, many scriptures abound emphasizing how God wants increase in the life of his people.

1 *"Hear therefore, O Israel, and observe to do it: that it may be well with thee, and that ye may increase mightily, as the LORD God of thy fathers hath promised thee, in the land that floweth with milk and honey." Deuteronomy 6:3*

2 *"Though thy beginning was small, yet thy latter end should greatly increase." Job 8:7*

3 *"Then shall the earth yield her increase; and God, even our own God, shall bless us." Psalms 67:6*

4   *"Yea, the LORD shall give that which is good; and our land shall yield her increase." Psalms 85:12*

5   *"The LORD shall increase you more and more, you and your children." Psalms 115:14*

6   *"And I will multiply upon you man and beast; and they shall increase and bring fruit: and I will settle you after your old estates, and will do better unto you than at the beginning: and ye shall know that I am the LORD." Ezekiel 36:11*

7   *"For the seed shall be prosperous; the vine shall give her fruit, and the ground shall hive her increase, and the heavens shall give her dew; and I will cause the remnant of this people to possess all these things." Zechariah 8:12*

Increase is on God's mind constantly in every area of your life God wants you to have an abundance of all things he wants to enlarge your borders and he is waiting on you to ask him to do.

"And Jabez called on the God of Israel, saying, Oh that thou wouldest bless me indeed, and enlarge my coast, and that thine hand might be

with me, and that thou wouldest keep me from evil, that it may not grieve me! And God granted him that which he requested." 1 Chronicles 4:10

Likewise God is ready to grant you your request for increase in your life he's ready to enlarge your coast and bless you indeed.

Words such as increase prosperity and wealth should be on your heart often for only when it is in your heart will you see it manifested in your life. *"For as he (man) thinketh in his heart, so is he." Proverbs 23:7*

- Financial freedom is your right you have a right to live a life where you have no problems paying your bills.

- You have a right to be able to have a new car in your driveway even two new cars.

- You have a right to own your own home and to be able to furnish it with the luxury amenities of life.

- You have a right to financial security in your money and have plenty of money in your account even after you have blessed others.

The word of God says *'Every man to whom God hath given riches and wealth, and hath given him power to eat thereof, and to take his portion, and to rejoice in his labour; this is the gift of God."* Ecclesiastes 5:19

Did you get that it said **"to whom God hath given riches and wealth"** not the devil, this tells me that God is interested in you having riches and wealth and desires that you be financially free.

The word of God abound with scriptures where God is trying to open our eyes to realize that financial freedom is a choice God has already ordained it for you it's yours.

In the book of Deuteronomy 28:1-14, God is emphasizing nothing but financial freedom if we obey his voice and keep his commandments and the main commandment is to love.

Look at these fourteen verses emphasizing financial freedom as God's will for your life.

1   *"God will set you on high above all nations of the earth"* ***Financial freedom.***

2   *"All these blessing shall come on thee, and overtake thee"* ***Financial freedom.***

3   *"Blessed shall thou be in the city, and blessed shalt thou be in field"* **Financial freedom**.

4   *"Blessed shall be the fruit of thy body, and the fruit of thy ground, and the fruit of thy cattle, the increase of thy kine, and the flocks of thy sheep"* **Financial freedom**.

5   *"Blessed shall be thy basket and thy store"* **Financial freedom**.

6   *"Blessed shall thou be when thou comest in, and blessed shalt thou be when thou goest out"* **Financial freedom.**

7   *"Your enemies shall be smitten before thy face and flee before thee seven ways"* *(God will fight your battles for you)* **Financial freedom.**

8   *"The LORD shall command the blessing upon thee in thy storehouses, in that which you set your hand unto, and he shall bless your land"* **Financial freedom.**

9   *"The LORD shall establish thee a holy people unto himself"* *(God's people that understand God's way shall have)* **Financial freedom**.

10 *"And all the people of the earth shall see that thou art called by the name of the LORD; and they shall be afraid of thee"* (because the hand of God is prospering your life) **Financial freedom.**

11 *"And the LORD shall make thee plenteous in goods"* **Financial freedom.**

12 *"And the LORD shall open unto thee his good treasure, and bless all the work of thine hand, thou shalt lend unto many nations, and thou shalt not borrow"* **Financial freedom.**

13 *"And the LORD shall make thee the head, and not the tail; and thou shalt be above only and thou shalt not be beneath"* **Financial freedom.**

14 *"And thou shalt not go aside from any of the words which I command thee this day, to the right hand, or to the left, to go after other gods to serve them"* (if you keep God's word and serve him only then you shall have) **Financial freedom.**

All of this is your rightful inheritance don't allow anyone to tell you that you should be more focused on spiritual things and forget about these natural things, they have no idea what spirit is speaking through them.

As Jesus spoke to Peter when he was trying to tell Jesus something contrary to the word of God, likewise you must realize that this person is not speaking the things of God when they tell you this.

Jesus said *"Get thee behind me, Satan: thou art an offense unto me: for thou savourest not the things that be of God, but those that be of men."* *Matthew 16:23*

Know that God is not telling you to only focus on spiritual things if this was so then he is refuting his own word according to 3 John 2, *" Beloved, I wish above all things that thou mayest prosper and be in health, even as thy soul prospereth.*

"God is not a man, that he should lie; neither the son of man, that he should repent: hath he said, and shall he not do it? Or hath he spoken, and shall he not make it good?" Numbers 23:19

17
Your Wealth Is In The Word

"This book of the law shall not depart out of thy mouth; but thou shalt meditate therein day and night, that thou mayest observe to do according to all that is written therein: for then thou shalt make thy way prosperous, and then thou shalt have good success." Joshua 1:8

The word of God is full of scriptures emphasizing how God wants his people to increase, prosper and have wealth. If you want to know what belongs to you get in the word of God, and find out what is rightfully yours as an heir of God.

Your wealth is in the word and the more of the word of God you get in you the more faith you're going to have to believe to acquire what belongs to you.

"So then faith cometh by hearing, and hearing by the word of God." Romans 10:17, Did you get that? Every Christian has been given *"the measure of faith,"* but it's up to you and I to increase that faith by hearing more of God's word.

Understand this, the word of God said *"faith cometh"* so there's no such thing as you not having the necessary faith needed to receive your increase, prosperity and wealth, if you would just hear more of the word of God then the needed faith will come.

Say it aloud, *"So then faith cometh by hearing, and hearing by the word of God."* If you want more faith then just hear more word not just once but continuously it didn't say faith cometh by having heard but by hearing meaning to hear over and over and over and over and over again.

• Your hearing of the word comes in a number of ways, you can continually hear as you listen to the word preached and taught.

• You can continually hear as you yourself speak the word of God in confessing the word out of your mouth.

• You can continually hear as you listen to

audio and videotapes of the preached and taught word.

- You can continually hear as you read the word of God on a continuous basis thereby getting the word of God in your spirit.

- You can continually hear as you meditate on the word of God.

There is no excuse for not hearing the word of God when you don't take out time to hear the word you're omitting an awesome power from helping you in life.

"For the word of God is quick (living, alive) and powerful (active) and sharper than any twoedged sword." Hebrews 4:12

You must begin to see the word of God in a different light you must begin to see that all your answers lie in the word of God, make it your business to have the attitude of David concerning God's word.

David spoke often of the love he had for God's word and how his help was in the word of God saying:

1   *"Blessed are the undefiled in the way, who walk in the law of the LORD.*

148

2   *Blessed are they that keep his testimonies, and that seek him with the whole heart.*

3   *Wherewithal shall a young man cleanse his way? by taking heed thereto according to thy word.*

4   *With my whole heart have I sought thee: O let me not wander from thy commandments.*

5   *I will meditate in thy precepts, and have respect unto thy ways. I will delight myself in thy statues: I will not forget thy word.*

6   *I opened my mouth, and panted: for I longed for thy commandments.*

7   *Rivers of waters run down mine eyes, because they keep not thy law." Psalms 119*

From this day forward, begin to make the word of God your priority, from this day forward find the word of God that fits your situation and meditate on it daily.

Go through the word of God and locate the scriptures that talks about increase, prosperity and wealth and meditate on these if you do this on a daily basis *"then thou shalt make thy way prosperous; and then thou shalt have good success." Joshua 1:8b*

God wants you to increase, prosper and have wealth and his word to you is *"Acquaint now thyself with him, and be at peace: thereby good shall come unto thee. Receive, I pray thee, the law from his mouth, and lay up his words in thine heart. If thou return to the Almighty, thou shalt be built up, thou shalt put away iniquity far from thy tabernacles.*

Then shalt thou lay up gold as dust, and the gold of Ophir as the stones of the brooks. Yea, the Almighty shall be thy defence, and thou shalt have plenty of silver.

For then shalt thou have thy delight in the Almighty, and shalt lift up thy face unto God. Thou shalt make thy prayer unto him, and he shall hear thee, and thou shalt pay thy vows.

Thou shalt also decree a thing, and it shall be established unto thee: and the light shall shine upon thy ways. When men are cast down, then thou shalt say, There is lifting up; and he shall save the humble person. He shall deliver the island of the innocent: and it is delivered by the pureness of thine hands." Job 22:

Go forth now and get your increase, prosperity and wealth for it's now awaiting your beckon and call as you allow your salary to work for you instead of against you.

A Word From the Heart
Of Dexter L. Jones

Thank you for your support in purchasing this book by you purchasing this book for your edification and knowledge you are likewise depositing into my life and giving me the opportunity to continue to write books that will bring about a change in the life of others.

Every life that this book touches you have played a part in it for you have enable me to continue to fulfill the mission and purpose that God has given me.

I appreciate you and will continue to keep you in my prayers that God will continually empower you to prosper according to his word. All my writings are for you it's my desire to bring to you the revelations and information that God gives to me that can help you in the financial game of life.

I understand that the financial realm is a hard realm in life to breakthrough but I know also that with God and the proper knowledge all things are possible. When I see the financial condition of people my eyes are like David's which said *"Rivers of water run down my eyes, (when I see the financial condition of people)" (inserted) Psalms 119:136*

I will not neglect and grow weary to bring to you every nugget of truth that God gives me that can bring about a change in your life. I will not rest until I have accomplished the will of God in bringing forth prosperity and financial truths that can cause you to increase.

I will not sugar coat or water down the word of prosperity for those who may persecute the prosperity message or those who are offended at my books that talks about money and increase. They haven't seen anything yet there's more to come.

God gets no pleasure in seeing one of his children struggle financially in life, no more than you would get pleasure in seeing your children struggle financially in life. The word of God says *"If ye then, being evil, know how to give good gifts unto your children, how much more shall your Father which is in heaven give good things to them that ask him?" Matthew 7:11*

My goal in writing books is not to give you a fish but a fishing pole and then teach you how to catch fishes for if I give you a fish you can only eat for a day but if I give you a pole and teach you how to use it you can fish at your pleasure and at will.

Well every book that God blesses me to write that book is your fishing pole and as you open the book therein lies the teaching of how to catch all the fishes you need to feed your family, yourself and others all the days of your life.

My heart is for you I'm in your corner I'm cheering you on daily praying for your financial increase, prosperity and wealth. Don't settle for less than a king's ransom for God has said, *"all things are yours."* **You can do it you can be rich!**

www.dexterjonesministries.org
millions737@yahoo.com

THE GREATEST WEALTH OF ALL

"And he spake a parable unto them, saying, The ground of a certain rich man brought forth plentifully: And he thought within himself, saying, What shall I do, because I have no room where to bestow my fruits? And he said, This will I do: I will pull down my barns, and build greater; and there will I bestow all my fruits and my goods. And I will say to my soul, Soul, thou hast much goods laid up for many years; take thine ease, eat, drink, and be merry. But God said unto him, Thou fool, this night thy soul shall be required of thee: then whose shall those things be, which thou hast provided? So is he that layeth up treasure for himself, and is not rich toward God." Luke 12:16-21

My desire is that you become financially wealthy but most of all that you become rich toward God. I desire to see you living the life of a dedicated and committed man or woman of God.

Drawing near to God as he draw near to you with a desire to pursue God and come into an intimate relationship with the Father.

As a man of God, I could not with all good conscience end this book without offering you the opportunity to receive the greatest wealth of all. All other wealth is pale in comparison to the riches of eternal life that belongs to you once you receive Jesus Christ as your Lord and Savior. It's simple really, you just ask Jesus to come into your life with this simple prayer.

"Dear God, according to your word I have sinned and come short of the glory of God. I stand in need of the Savior Jesus Christ. I repent of my sins and ask Jesus to come into my life, I acknowledge that I am a sinner and need to be saved. I believe that Jesus died, were resurrected and is now alive at your right hand. I ask that the blood of Jesus cleanse me from all sins and I accept Jesus into my life now. Father I thank you for receiving me, I am now a child of God, I'm saved and my name is written in the lambs book of life, in Jesus name, Amen."

Tell us about your decision in receiving Jesus Christ as your Lord and Savior, we will get you out some literature as soon as possible, God bless you and keep you.

100% Guaranteed Pain Relief
"Feel the Thrill of a Pain Free Life"

Jones' All Natural Australian Oil of Eucalyptus

SAY GOOD-BYE TO YOUR ACHES, PAINS AND SORENESS!

Upper and lower back pain, shoulder, knee and all body aches, Arthritis, Emphysema, Sinus and Sinus Headaches, Asthma, Pains and Soreness. Rheumatism, Colds, Gout, Hay Fever, Bruises, Insect Bites, Burns and Sunburns, Chest Congestion, Bronchitis, Rashes, Cold Sores and Carpal Tunnel Syndrome, FibroMyalgia and much more.

An incredible All Natural Product, that you simply rub on the affected area and begin to receive immediate relief from your aches, pains and respiratory problems.

Send or call today for a **FREE WEEK SUPPLY TRIAL SIZE** of this incredible product and begin to live a better quality of life. Simply pay shipping charges of $4.95 and receive your product right away.

FEEL BETTER INTERPRISE
1-919-273-3195 or www.dexterjonesministries.org
email: millions737@yahoo.com

Printed in the United States
51615LVS00001B/34-135

9 781600 470233